FM AGILE V2-20.3

I0032171

AGILE V2

COACH'S FIELD MANUAL

JAMES K SMITH

INCREASE SIGNAL CORPORATION

Increase Signal

ISBN: 978-1-7358581-2-8
Kindle ISBN: 978-1-7358581-0-4
eBook ISBN: 978-1-7358581-1-1

For information about permission to reproduce selections from this book, email to permissions@increasesignal.com

Cover, book design, images, figures, and callouts by James K Smith.

For information about special discounts for bulk purchases, or for information on seminars, training, or consulting, please visit IncreaseSignal.com

FOREWORD

I'm a great believer in the Japanese martial art concept of *shuhari*, which describes the stages of learning from initial exposure to mastery.

Put in terms of agility and business systems, we need a concept of learning that is in the same spirit, but more rigorous, descriptive and less subject to easy interpretation; qualities often missing from our agile conversations. With that in mind, let's explore.

As coaches and consultants, we tend to first *Emulate* the processes we learn, applying basic Kanban, Scrum and scaling frameworks as faithfully as we can, given how we were taught, often via certifications.

Practice and repetition are key, leading us to the next level called *Embrace* – the state of understanding why the processes and frameworks are designed to execute the way they do.

Emulate and Embrace provide the answer to that worn out interview question regarding *"what's the difference between being agile and doing agile ?"* so if you get nothing else from this book, at least you'll have the answer to that question if asked during an interview.

Emulate then Embrace is a concept that implies a flow of lesser to greater understanding, which characterizes so much of our work as agile coaches and business systems engineers. It is our most elemental design thinking; our journey through the *"cone of uncertainty,"* and represents two important statuses on the Kanban board of life.

That leads us to the third fundamental stage in lean-agile thinking, which is *Establish.* The concept of Establish implies having the understanding and experience to *innovate* and *improve*, which done *continuously*, is an agile value, along with trust, transparency, and commitment. We know the process, and have certifications to prove it, but now we understand the process and why it executes the way it does. Now, as agile coaches, we must improve the process to eliminate wasted time and effort and increase efficiency – *to simplify and practice economy of flow.* And the flow continues, even with the learning progression. What we Establish is the invitation for others to Emulate, just as we did.

And that's exactly why we as coaches help organizations become more efficient. Just as with martial artists, we have applied the years of practice and rigor required to know and understand processes, so that we can improve and simplify our clients' business systems. Not unlike **shuhari,** it's important not to take the first two stages of agile learning (*Emulate, Embrace*) for granted, and assume we can jump straight to practicing the innovation of the *Establish* stage. If we do, we'll likely get our butts kicked.

So know your Scrum and Kanban processes inside and out, study the scaling frameworks thoroughly, and understand why they include the rigor they do. Understand how to turn agile values into agile habits. Practice that *rigor, repeat, re-measure*. Knowledge and fundamental application lead us to our own, leaner ways of execution yielding better outcomes – that's the expression of continuous improvement in our chosen profession.

The frameworks, the half dozen or so certifications we all have, the coaching of behaviors, and even the agile transformation industry itself are all part of what I like to call Agile V1. But in our journey beyond Agile V1, what have we distilled in our understanding?

It's this: What organizations are trying to do is just have an efficient conversation that may start out with a bunch of noise, but will eventually generate enough signal that can be executed on to create value.

There's no magic in generating this signal, and no complicated math; it's reinforced by simplicity, teams, and rhythm leading to a balance of flow. That's what I'm going to examine in this book: templates, techniques and team topologies that facilitate the organizational conversation to produce value in the simplest possible way. That is the essence of Agile V2.

James K Smith
Miami Beach
August 25, 2020

TABLE OF CONTENTS

APPENDIX

Palm trees on Miami Beach, Oct 13, 2020

ACKNOWLEDGMENTS

Many thanks to teams and mentor-coaches who provided inspiration for the templates and techniques illustrated in this book. A special mention goes out to a handful of coaches who helped me understand the value of system of transformation guardrails, why the ability to map strategy to tactics is critical, why Kanban is the embodiment of flow, and the real power of Scrum as a delivery process that provides certainty and predictability. I also want to recognize a lot of great people at world-class organizations like Ford Motor and CSX. Companies like these who already maintain a strong sense of stewardship in their corporate culture make my job a hell of a lot easier.

My commitment to creativity, innovation, quality and engineering craftsmanship was heavily instilled in me by my tenure at many small "shrink-wrapped software" companies. If you want to sharpen your skills as a software developer, work for a small company whose survival depends solely on the quality of, and innovation in its software products.

Credit goes to Ken Rubin for some of the graphics in this book. Treat his classic , "Essential Scrum" as mandatory reading.

SECTION 1
THE AGILE V2 MINDSET

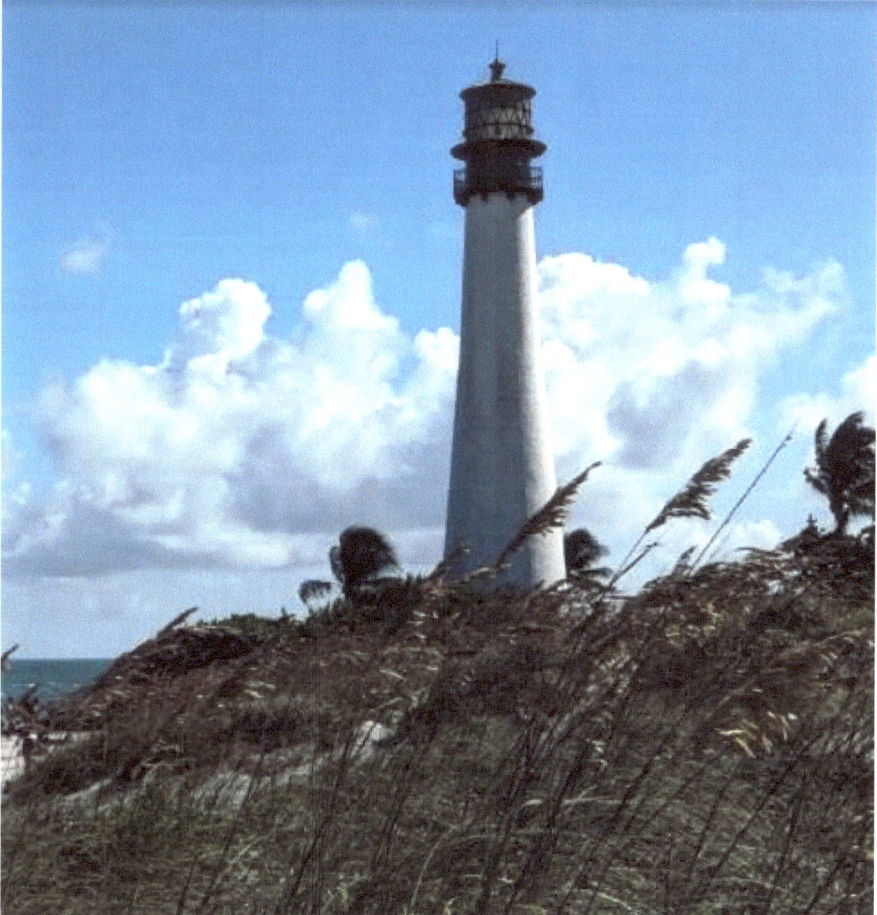

Cape Florida, August 27, 2020

CHAPTER 1
SIMPLIFY TO IMPROVE

The way organizations deliver value is heavily influenced by their communication structure. This thesis is known as Conway's Law. Oftentimes it's the case with organizations using inefficient delivery systems full of communication gaps.

Here's an example: A common, simplistic way to structure an organization delivering value is to create a bunch of functional silos as teams, organized and managed by a hierarchical structure.

The reason this organizational structure can be so inefficient, is because these siloed teams are missing communication channels that allow them to identify healthy and unhealthy dependencies, duplication of effort, efficient customer intake, and lean management of organizational budget. Additionally, these missing channels encourage unnecessarily heavy cognitive and communication loads on the teams. They end up having to do everything, from identifying strategic initiatives, to elaborating on these initiatives well enough to successfully execute on them within a competitive time frame.

So the answer to this quandary has been to institute in organizations what many have called the "Inverse Conway Maneuver." In *Accelerate: The Science of Lean Software and Dev Ops*, the authors suggest that:

*Our research lends support to what is sometimes called the **"inverse Conway maneuver,"** which states that organizations should evolve their team and organizational structure to achieve the desired architecture. The* *goal is for your architecture to support the ability of teams to get their work done – from design through to deployment – without requiring high-bandwidth communication between teams.*

People who identified this issue also identified a market. They came up with, for all intents, *"inverse Conway"* frameworks, and monetized these efforts with consulting and certifications. The expectation is that the organizations that adopt these out-of-box communication systems will realize increased efficiency.

Besides force-fitting your organization into a communication framework, another problem with this approach is that it doesn't make much accommodation for keeping your organizational delivery system as simple as possible. Simple systems are easier and cheaper to train, improve, operate, and respond to change. ***Don't add complexity unless that complexity is worth the dysfunction it addresses.***

So just providing a "**one size fits all**" agile framework to your clients then asking them to assemble the parts under your guidance, and then turn on the resulting machine doesn't always work that well. To account for this limitation, one provider even offers multiple options (complexities) of the same out-of-box framework. With this approach, at least the organization has some choice in the complexity it's willing to take on – except that every option still makes use of (for example) a PI planning event. We can't distill the process enough that we are able to deprecate this stressful, stop-the-world event in favor of continuous planning?

This approach the agile industry provides certainly hasn't changed much. It's what I like to call Agile V1, and is a fair representation of leaving us stuck in the *Emulate* stage in what I've been calling the

Emulate, Embrace, Establish learning progression:

Emulate: We learn the rules and best practices, and apply these learnings with limited understanding. We coach delivery performance as driven by the checklists of others.

Embrace: Experience leads to guiding our actions based on understanding of rules and best practices. We display increasing ability to identify situational dysfunction and provide solutions. We begin to modify our delivery performance checklists.

Establish: Experience and understanding are rich enough that use of rules and best practices becomes implicit. Logic replaces the rules. Connecting situations and determining actions becomes intuitive. "Smells" yield faster data than checklists. Performance is achieved via independent observations on delivery proficiency, rhythm, balance of flow, and outcomes instead of canned solutions. Only now can you replace Chesterton's fence with your own.

Suggesting these scaling frameworks represent Agile V1 isn't a slight. We all had to go through the throes and rigor of emulation to achieve understanding. The existing agile frameworks aren't casual efforts – they're the result of experts following their own *EEE* journey for years. Experienced scholars who have written books on process flow, understand how to measure value production and design organizational systems are substantial contributors to these frameworks.

So there's an incredible wealth of general knowledge to be gained by achieving certifications in these frameworks, and they should not be discounted. More importantly, as coach and systems engineer you need to understand why these frameworks are structured the way they are to progress through the *EEE* flow of this discipline yourself.

The problem is, the authors of these frameworks need you to perpetually stay in the *Emulation* of Agile V1. That's how they make money through certification and consulting fees.

So we keep *emulating*, and wait for the framework authors to determine the improvements for the next framework version. Then the accompanying certifications are updated, so as agile coaches, we must re-certify to keep our certifications current.

All this stagnation has caused much associated baggage as well. The three most popular backlog tools, TFS, Jira, and Rally sufficiently accommodate the out-of-box agile frameworks and Agile V1 approaches, so they have little incentive to improve either. Nothing innovative has come from work-item refinement efforts in years. In *Chapter 11*, I'll illustrate a backlog taxonomy that Agile V1 tools and frameworks don't even support. Ah, the ironic revenge of whiteboards and spreadsheets, when lean-agile systems thinking loses its commitment to innovation.

So while we tell our clients about the importance of following their own *EEE* journey, we don't adopt it ourselves as we should. So *Embrace*, then *simplify to Establish.* That's often the result of continuous improvement. Eliminate the waste in your thinking. Distill your understanding as you search for your own Agile V2. ***Innovation awaits your discovery.***

CHAPTER 2
THE CONVERSATION

Think about the delivery systems your organization uses to provide value to the intended customer. The systems are what frame the starting point of an effort that could include concepts, initiatives and hypotheses. As the system progresses, information and knowledge lead to actions. And at the endpoint of the system, the actions have produced something marketable. Could be a car or service, or a chocolate cake.

Whatever is produced, in its simplest form, is just a conversation that originally started out with discussion around what is desired as an outcome and how we get to that outcome.

How lucrative that outcome will be depends heavily on how the conversation is structured. As Dean Leffingwell suggests, conversations, hopefully for better and not for worse, start with "strategic opinions" and end with "**executable facts**."

Does the conversation include a way to vet ideas early, so they can be tossed quickly if necessary? Does the conversation support a flow to executable facts that is optimal for the conversation given the available resources? Is the conversation efficient enough to develop value as quickly as the conversations your competitors are having?

The organizational conversation is such a simple concept, but the result of that conversation could have massive consequences. That's a notion that most organizations grasp, and painfully so. They simply want organizational conversations that yield better outcomes with less waste along the way. Thus, the appetite for business systems analysis, agile frameworks, and coaches who can help organizations implement those frameworks - even if it means those organizations may have to radically transform their operations along the way, taking years to complete.

But remember, we're still just talking about a conversation. So with this simplified perspective, does the organizational conversation still require a complex framework to improve delivery? Does the organization even need to undergo some large transformation to just have this efficient conversation? Maybe, but let's make sure the simple stuff is covered first.

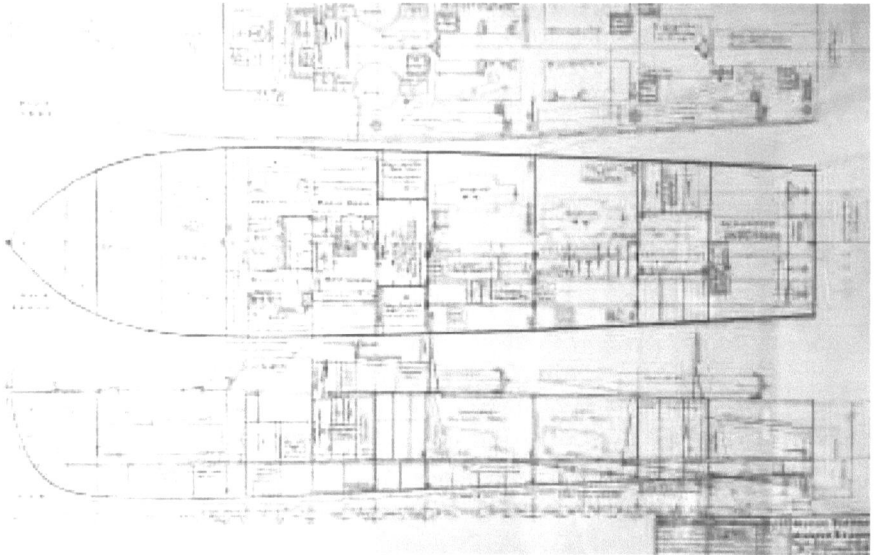

Original drawing of a Motor Torpedo Boat, dated June 30, 1941 and designed by Frank Pembroke Huckins. His company, Huckins Yacht Corporation was one of three manufacturers selected to design and build PT Boats during WWII. Taken at Huckins Corp Office, Jacksonville, Florida Sept. 1, 2020.

CHAPTER 3
SO WHERE IS THIS CONVERSATION YOU SPEAK OF?

It's right in front of us; it's just hard to see because of all those Agile V1 details and fundamentals we had to learn to help us visualize the conversation in full. And that's ok, since, in classic *EEE* fashion, our path has to take us through the trees before we get to the other side of the forest to understand the forest as a whole.

We now *Embrace* what agile frameworks are attempting to achieve, and by what means. Stop just *embracing* and start *Establishing. Distill, Simplify, Improve,* given organizational requirements and resources. That's Agile v2.

We have conceptual starts (strategic opinions) and ends (executable facts) to the conversation. That's half the effort right there. Now we just have to fill out the middle of the conversation to make it effective, just like the frameworks do. But before we go to all the expense, effort, and time that frameworks require, let's start out with something much simpler.

In the spirit of discovery, let's nibble at this problem, beginning with this question: what does it take to steward the organizational conversation in a way that it ideally continuously delivers more signal and less noise? Think of it like this. The DevOps notion of CI/CD actually starts at the strategic opinion level, and not at the delivery level. An efficient conversation should both continuously integrate signal while continuously delivering less noise over time. Along the way, that signal will take on a physical form as defined by what the organization thinks its value is. Let's visualize a simple conversation progression using the Cone of Uncertainty.

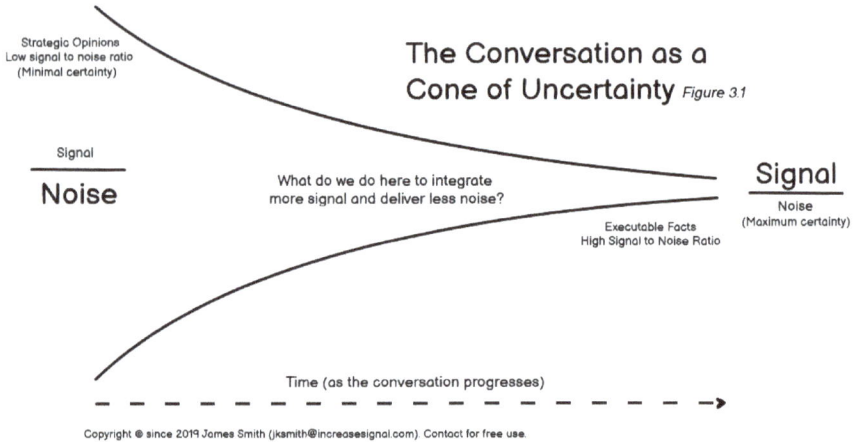

The Conversation as a Cone of Uncertainty Figure 3.1

This progression is also an outcome of design thinking by another name. I'm not clear on why coaches hold design thinking workshops as if design thinking is some kind of new approach. This is how we always conceptualize a design process. And the outcome is simple; increase the signal to noise value as the conversation progresses. The Design Squiggle is a brilliantly simple expression of this concept.

The remainder of this manual is dedicated to illustrating techniques for generating that signal. Conceptualize without the heavy framework machinery; for the sake of a robust and healthy conversation, as I've said before, don't add complexity to a system if that complexity is not worth the dysfunction or waste it addresses.

For example, do you need a complex work-item taxonomy with lots of runway? Maybe, but don't hesitate to start with something simpler. Do you need PI (or as my colleagues call it, Big Room) planning as a default? Perhaps, but be sure to prove that assertion via the efficiency of the conversation first. Do you need to have a big yarn party on the wall to track dependencies? Maybe, but those things look like painful eye charts and maybe you can deprecate their value by including conversations about dependencies just at the right alignment points all along the conversation.

Until we actually had to do PI planning and use a variety of other framework techniques did we realize that we're just trying to have a productive organizational conversation. Whether it's a conversation on behalf of a Fortune 10 company with 500k employees, or a bakery making chocolate cakes, in the end, it's just a structured conversation.

Miami skyline, Aug. 28, 2020 Miami, Florida

CHAPTER 4
THE CONVERSATION STRUCTURE

Frameworks at a minimum tell us what our team topologies should be and what our work-item taxonomies that those teams will execute on should look like. Fundamental inverse Conway activities. But now that we understand this, we can help organizations determine their own topographies and taxonomies without the defaults. Instead of people forcing process or process forcing people, work with people to help them structure a conversation that works best to deliver value for their organization.

Let's start with delivery teams. If the executable facts our teams reveal all share a single budget, that's a challenge. That means delivery teams will be fighting over budget in probably unhealthy ways. Also, the delivery teams certainly don't want to duplicate the effort required to determine these facts, as that equates to waste in our delivery system. Management wait states are another system waste, so we want our conversation to encourage pushing the planning of work as close as possible to the teams actually doing the work. That's the most efficient approach to use of resources in our conversation.

But doing so comes with its own set of issues. Why not just set up some teams, prioritize our strategic opinions, and then hand off these opinions to the delivery teams to turn them into facts? We can track shared use of the common budget and ask the teams in "Scrum of Scrums" fashion to discuss their work with each other for the sake of identifying dependencies and duplicated work.

That kind of organizational conversation addresses basic needs, but it doesn't scale well. Further, it's unlikely that a delivery team can use a single process to sufficiently elaborate the conversation to produce enough actionable signal in a reasonable (competitive) amount of time. Large scale conversations would force delivery teams doing all the work to handle too many communication channels (that's as bad as too few) and too much cognitive load – a sure-fire recipe that leads to negatively impacting team performance and disrupting the flow of value.

If your delivery teams believe they can be responsible for producing that much signal in the conversation, let them give it a try. But to be more successful, it's likely they'll want their scope to be more limited.

So the hypothesis for our conversation structure is beginning to take shape. Delivery teams won't get the whole whale to eat, but just a portion of the whale they can consume with high confidence. That's exactly what we want from our delivery teams – an efficient conversation depends on teams who are provided enough signal that lets them deliver with high confidence. That amount of signal meets their definition that specifies their readiness to go to work. And continuing with the whale-eating idiom, delivery teams tend to consume the whale best (with confidence) if their bites are the size of *stories and tasks* (see upcoming lexicon).

So how do we get the conversation to the point that it produces enough signal that satisfies their definition of ready?

That happens in that part of the conversation that takes place prior to delivery. Now is a good time to start creating a lexicon around conversation structure.

Miami Beach, August 26, 2020

CHAPTER 5
LEXICON

Signal: Information content at a particular point in the conversation.

Noise: Lack of information at a particular point in the conversation.

Signal/Noise Ratio: Measure of Signal vs Noise at any particular point in the conversation.

Taxonomy: a hierarchical classification of actionable content in a delivery system specific to the conversation.

Alignment Point: A point in the conversation specifically inserted to facilitate increasing signal/noise ratio and allowing the pull of work through the conversation. The output of the last alignment point in the flow is ultimately delivered to the customer. Alignment Point facilitation is enabled by one or more teams.

Flow: The continuous, measurable delivery of increasing value in the conversation. Alignment Points are used to make the flow more efficient, and have fewer constraints.

Team Topology: Structure of teams used to facilitate Alignment Points in the conversation.

Cognitive Load: The intrinsic bandwidth load associated with team scope of work.

Communication Load: The impact of the effort required to send and receive messages by the team.

Holding Cost: Cost reflecting a team's cognitive and communication load. Too much load makes costs rise.

Transaction Cost: Cost reflecting the team's process effort to get work done. Think administration and lack of automation. If cognitive load is low and transaction cost is high, work batch sizes may need to be adjusted, or the chosen process is simply too costly.

Cycle Time: Total time from beginning to end of process for a work-item. Multiple work-item cycle times can be used to calculate an average process cycle time.

Lead Time: Total time from when work begins at a particular alignment point (or work-item) to when a resulting product is delivered to the customer.

Flow Efficiency: The ratio of active time for a work-item to the active+wait+hold time for the same work-item.

Cycle time, Lead time, and Flow Efficiency provide valuable information for managing *Holding Cost and Transaction Cost* and optimizing conversation *Flow, Cognitive Load, and Communication Load*.

To complete our lexicon, let's continue with the whale-eating idiom by framing the size of the possible bites. The following work-item descriptions are common in what you'd see in typical backlog tools such as Jira, TFS, and Rally. The sizing guidelines are nothing more than suggestions.

Epic: Connects strategy to customers and markets. Could require 1+ years to complete.

Sub-Epic: (or Capability): Connects customers and markets to problems. A small sub-epic might require two quarters, medium three quarters, large four quarters.

Feature: Connects problems to solutions. Features need to fit inside a release. Whatever you define as a release should be radiated in a release map or Product Roadmap. Depending on the release pipeline, many actual customer releases may have happened by the time a release milestone is reached in the roadmap.

Story: Connects solutions to execution. If stories are executed in Scrum, they will be completed in a single iteration.

There are other work-item descriptions we'll be using at the Investment level, as described in *Chapter 11*. So, armed with our lexicon, let's finish building out our sample conversation structure.

CHAPTER 6
MORE CONVERSATION STRUCTURE

Instead of being responsible for the whole organizational conversation, delivery teams tend to be more effective if they continue the conversation once it has the requisite signal for them to execute with high confidence. Can whatever the rest of the conversation is, be handled by an additional alignment point in front of the delivery team?

Maybe, but let's try out some scope. I've seen teams working at the portfolio alignment point effectively produce epics, sub-epics, and features to provide enough signal that the delivery teams can consume and execute with confidence. This alignment point often manages prioritization and sequencing, 3rd party system integrators and suppliers, adjusting lean budget, as well as identification of risks and dependencies.

For alignment points using Kanban (see *Chapter 9*), it's important to check flow efficiency and cycle time at each of these alignment points to determine efficiency and adjust conversation structure accordingly. So, assuming the scope batch of this portfolio alignment point is properly sized, let's review what our conversation structure is.

We have two general alignment point definitions as part of our conversation structure. One handles distillation of conversation signal that suggests solutions, and along the way, identifies risks and dependencies, manages system integrators, prioritizes and sequences work, and adjusts budget. We're calling this the Portfolio alignment point. The other takes the signal that represents broad solutions, and refines those solutions into any number of work-items that can be executed on and delivered to the customer. We're calling this the Delivery alignment point. As with the portfolio alignment point, there may be many teams representing this delivery alignment point.

Ok, not bad. But let's ask ourselves, does the conversation have any *potential* waste we haven't identified? Maybe, and it may require some iterating of the conversation to see that waste. What about gaps in the conversation that haven't been filled with signal?

That depends. The conversation taxonomy represents an inventory runway. If the runway is too short, then it's likely signal will come crashing into an alignment point down the flow, and that alignment point will become overloaded (watch holding costs spike at that level). If the runway is too long, then people tend to gratuitously introduce unnecessary make-work for a particular work-item type. Also transaction cost goes up. That's a system waste.

So let's dig into this a bit more by examining the epic work-item. Do epics already expect some signal to exist in the conversation, or can they originate signal as the conversation is just getting started?

Again, flow efficiency and cycle-time measurements could reveal some guidance surrounding epic refinement. Do we even need a runway that includes epics? If we do need epic work-items, what about go/no go, proof of concept, market fit analysis, long-term leadership fit analysis, and sunk cost tolerance guardrails for strategic opinions? Are these included in epic work-item scope, or do they make the scope too large or confused?

If you need investment guardrails in place, or by measuring flow it's determined that holding costs are too high at the epic level, this may require one additional alignment point very early, or even at the beginning of the organizational conversation. Let's call it an investment alignment point.

So let's see where these alignment points might be located in our conversation as represented by the Cone of Uncertainty:

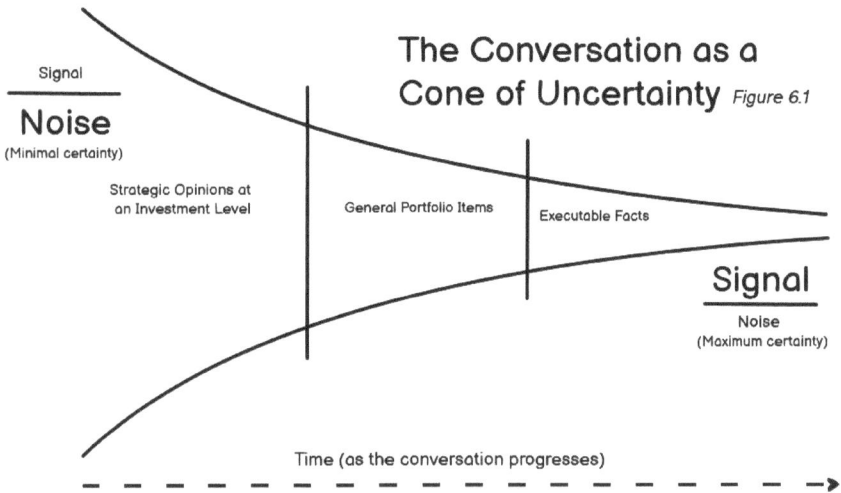

The Conversation as a Cone of Uncertainty *Figure 6.1*

Signal / Noise (Minimal certainty)

Strategic Opinions at an Investment Level — General Portfolio Items — Executable Facts

Signal / Noise (Maximum certainty)

Time (as the conversation progresses)

CHAPTER 7
MASTERY, AUTONOMY, PURPOSE

So, now that we have an organizational conversation with three alignment points, let's review. Conway's law tells us our delivery system will be forced to model our organizational interactions and communications. But these interactions and communications may be far less than efficient, perhaps even anti-competitive.

Our response is to do an inverse Conway maneuver. That is, reorganize communications and interactions into delivery systems. Existing agile frameworks provide a canned system for that purpose, and what I like to call Agile V1. As we walk along our *Emulate, Embrace, Establish* path, it necessarily requires going through developing and iterating over V1 before we have the understanding to develop Agile V2.

Besides making use of agile frameworks, Agile V1 also waves banners displaying the value of people over processes, servant leadership, and team autonomy, as if they had value in and of themselves (the human element of agility). The harsh reality is, those banners only have value in their ability to enhance conversation *flow* for the benefit of the organization (of people). People collaborate via process to get things done. Want humans to work together more efficiently? Don't force them into using a delivery system they don't maintain themselves - provide them the freedom to, as Daniel Pink identified, practice Mastery, Autonomy, and Purpose.

So how do we facilitate mastery, autonomy, and purpose for the sake of a more effective delivery system? The effort doesn't require the services of a team counselor. That's another Agile V1 artifact. It simply requires that a delivery system be identified that efficiently pushes the decision making as close as possible to the people delivering the outcomes. A system that encourages this produces higher engagement, leading to better decisions, and faster execution.

The Project Manager's Infinite Loop

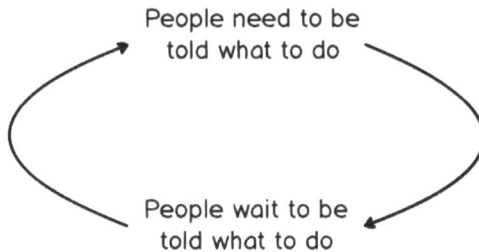

People need to be
told what to do

People wait to be
told what to do

Copyright 2019 James K Smith (jksmith@dkxagile.com) Contact for free use

Mastery, autonomy, and purpose are a by-product of this execution strategy. So, directly coaching the human side of agility as an end in and of itself is a distraction. To cultivate the best environment for happy, fulfilled, high-performing teams, codify mastery, autonomy, and purpose right into an organizational conversation that is designed to *push the planning of work as close as possible to the people doing the work, given their capacity.*

At this point we've modeled the high-level view of an effective conversation that we propose can deliver value for the organization. Our hypothesis is that this conversation structure has potential to not only address the weaknesses in the organizational delivery system Conway's law identifies, but also does this without forcing organizational conversations and interactions into a packaged framework. But that's just the hypothesis.

What can we do to test this hypothesis? Time to build a measurable execution strategy around our conversation, comprised of Investment, Portfolio, and Delivery alignment points.

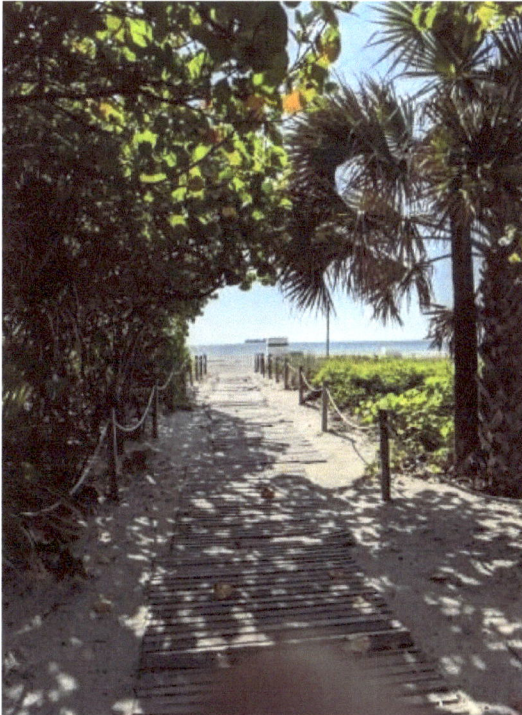

Beach entry from Miami Beach Boardwalk, May 20, 2020

SECTION 2
REALIZING AGILE V2 EXECUTION STRATEGY

Miami Beach Boardwalk, August 25, 2020

CHAPTER 8
WHAT IS A SYSTEM OF DELIVERY?

So we've talked about the organizational conversation. To operationalize the conversation, people need structure and processes that support an optimal flow of information. Such an execution strategy gives the organization the greatest opportunity for delivering the best value-driven outcomes.

To facilitate, we've identified some team alignment points. We will identify some techniques and templates that help teams at these alignment points execute for the benefit of increasing signal.

But that's not all a good execution strategy should include. While processes and structure should be continuously optimized to maintain competitiveness, this optimization is wholly driven by the intent of the people operating the delivery system realized from the execution strategy. The values the operators of the system maintain will determine if the strategy is a flop or an execution powerhouse.

So any execution strategy should be anchored by a *cultural contract*.

"Culture eats Strategy for Breakfast" - Drucker
"Yeah, but Strategy that Codifies Culture is Like Eggs and Bacon" - James

This cultural contract should state: *The delivery system will be designed and improved to show reciprocation of the agile values (trust, transparency, commitment, and continuous improvement), and will implement flow that represents mastery, autonomy, and purpose.*

Organizational Working Agreement

Except when necessary for security or governance reasons, the entire organization will at least have "read-only" visibility into the organizational conversation. This includes objectives and evidence that the cultural contract is being met at all conversation alignment points.

Let's define these agile values:

Trust – in the system and in the operators running the system. A system that reciprocates trust executes in a leaner fashion.

Transparency – Visibility into, and understanding of, any part of the system. The operators hide nothing. By contract, operate the system as designed without any fear of reprisal from the organization. Transparency must be applied given organizational constraints, such as need to know, security or process governance. Examples would be separation of UAT and production data due to HIPAA requirements, or process controls in place due to SSAE 16 requirements. In these cases, transparency in the delivery system will be domain specific.

Commitment – Commitment to enabling the system as a whole to deliver value. That's the driver for continuous improvement. Another application of commitment involves the nature of the work being done - commitment increases as signal in the conversation increases. Execution commitment is low at the strategic opinion stage of the conversation, but is very high at the stage where execution of facts occurs. Teams that execute on solutions must be willing to commit to completing increments of value on cadence. Otherwise, the system has no reliable delivery mechanism.

Continuous Improvement – Continuous improvement is part of an organization's survival strategy. A good delivery system has built-in mechanisms for identifying waste, strategic refactoring, and therefore continuous improvement.

There's a crucially key word used in our cultural contract: *reciprocation*. Borrowing from security system design, *reciprocation occurs when objectives are identified and, in the course of execution, evidence is produced to show that those objectives have been met.*

So how do we make reciprocation happen? By codifying agile values (the objectives), and evidence the values are being practiced directly in the system of delivery.

Agile values can be introduced by coaching, classroom training, and agile games. But the way to make agile values actionable, is by codifying them into the delivery system. Doing so enables agile values to become *habits*. And if agile values become habits, all the operators of the delivery system have to do is simply *trust and follow the process* itself. The result is a more efficient delivery system, since operator focus has been distilled and simplified. In chapters to come, we will examine mechanisms that illustrate reciprocation of all the agile values.

Execution of cultural values through the delivery system is core to any organizational execution strategy. Additional crucial values identified include Daniel Pink's *mastery, autonomy, and purpose,* which are by-products of an execution strategy that pushes the planning of work as close as possible to the people delivering the work. This is what "servant leadership" is, and nothing more.

Agile Culture v1 (explicit, subjective, difficult to measure):
"People over processes."
"Servant leadership."
"Mastery, autonomy, and purpose."

Agile Culture v2 (implicit, objective, easier to measure):
"The Most Successful Execution Strategies Operationalize
a Cultural Contract. All that V1 stuff is built in."

Let's take a look at various processes, techniques and templates that facilitate codifying agile values as well as increase signal and decrease noise in the organizational conversation.

Main mast from the schooner Columbia, August 13 2020, Panama City, FL

CHAPTER 9
PROCESSES FOR INCREASING SIGNAL IN THE CONVERSATION

We will be focusing specifically on two processes, Kanban and Scrum. Their efficacy should be considered given the amount of signal that is available at the beginning of the process and the increased amount of signal we hope to achieve at the end of the process.

Additionally, we need a process at the execution stage of our conversation that *reciprocates* commitment with heavy emphasis on certainty of delivery. Here's a graphic I use in my Agile 101 slide deck:

Comparison of Scrum and Kanban Processes *Figure 9.1*

Scrum	Kanban
High administration but simpler.	Greater flexibility but potentially more complicated.
Commitments expected to complete work in one sprint	Does not require work being done in a particular increment of time.
Work Items are relative size estimated and require more grooming.	Anything described as a "unit of work" can be put on board.
Process requires up front preparation.	Requires no preparation.
Works best for 5-9 team resources.	Can work with any size team.
Easy to execute.	Can become complicated to execute when dealing with multiple value streams and optimizing workflow.
Works great for greenfield development.	Can be used for any kind work but doesn't have the same throughput as Scrum.
The process itself takes on the responsibility for getting work done.	Responsibility for getting work done rests with specific resources doing the work.
Emphasis on whole team as the asset.	Emphasis on resources vs work needing to be done.
Primary measurement is Velocity.	Measured by Cycle Time and Flow Efficiency.
Scrum Board has 3 columns (To do, In Progress, Done).	Kanban board designed to support required workflow.

Kanban is simply an inventory control process that can be measured. The process is comprised of a number of statuses that represent the flow of a work-item, from typically the starting status "To Do" to an ending status "Done." Each Kanban board that is used in any part of the system of delivery represents in and of itself a miniature system of delivery. Given the flexibility of Kanban, depending on its design, it is suitable for providing a general process that can effectively deliver more signal, no matter where it is placed in the organizational conversation.

Kanban's flexibility also comes at a price. Complete certainty that Kanban can deliver on cadence is not guaranteed. The reason why is that Kanban is designed to accommodate multiple work-item statuses that can each have a variable processing speed over any measurement interval.

Envision the Kanban process as a pipe having multiple diameters to accommodate flow content that changes over time. So, to adjust statuses by identifying constraints and wait-states, process measurements such as cycle-time and flow efficiency are employed. What we hope to achieve with these measurements is an optimal process flow through the pipe given the constraints in the nature of the work in the flow – buffer the pipe where possible. Here's another graphic from my Agile 101 class:

Kanban Board

Figure 9.2

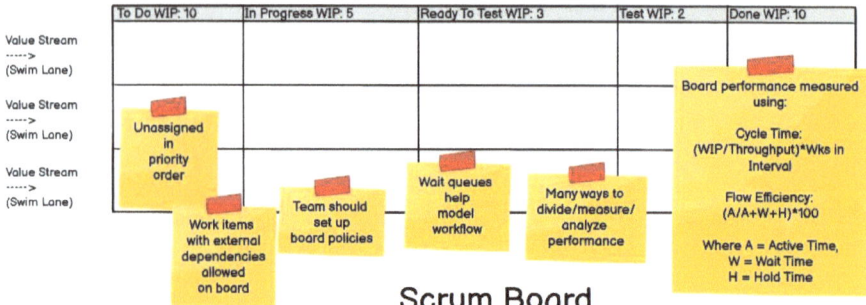

Scrum Board

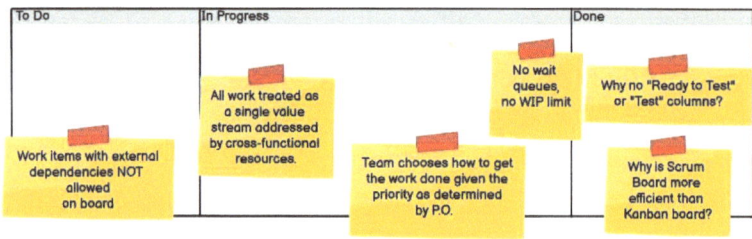

To increase confidence that value will be delivered predictably on cadence, use Scrum. Scrum is the simplest Kanban process with just one status speed. In the broad sense that speed is always one iteration. Scrum is capable of fully completing every work-item in its pipe on a regular cadence, but to do so, it needs proper administration, volume of flow, and enough signal in the conversation so work-items meet the Definition of Ready for the Scrum team. Whenever the conversation simply does not have enough signal to be considered executable within a specific cadence, use Scrum's parent, which is Kanban.

In the system with our proposed alignment points, Investment and Portfolio will use the Kanban process. Delivery will make use of the Scrum process. Kanban can certainly be used at the delivery alignment point as well, but generally only when signal levels cannot be guaranteed to be deliverable on cadence, or on-demand work is required. For a Scrum process even more bulletproof than what we learn in our certifications, I'll provide some valuable structure to Scrum in *Chapter 17. Ceremony Templates for High Performance Scrum Teams.*

Exercise Questions:

1) In *Figure 9.2*, how many constraint buffers does the Kanban board have versus the Scrum board? (Read up on constraint buffers and Theory of Constraints).

2) Why is Scrum always expected to have a cycle-time of one iteration and a flow efficiency of 100%? (*refer to Figure 9.2*).

3) Why should your Scrum board not have a "Ready to Test" or "Test" status?

4) Bonus question: How would you describe "holding costs" and "transaction (administrative) costs" for each process? Check out this video on optimal batch sizes for clues.

Jacksonville Beach, Florida, August 31, 2020

CHAPTER 10
THE PORTFOLIO RUNWAY AND NOTES ON TEMPLATE USE

The current crop of backlog tools support use of epics, sub-epics, and features as portfolio work-items. These work-items as a taxonomy could be called the portfolio *runway*.

Considerations about the portfolio runway can be very strategic – too long of a runway makes some work become gratuitous (and therefore wasteful). If the taxonomy is repeating the same signal from epic to sub-epic, or from sub-epic to feature, maybe the runway is too long. Epics might be better used as simple division containers. Perhaps sub-epics can be used as simple product containers.

On the other hand, for complex organizations with many alignment considerations, a full epic, sub-epic, and feature taxonomy is employed. An indicator that the portfolio runway is too short for this more complex organization occurs when features provided to delivery teams are still so broad in scope or lacking in signal that delivery team execution speed is negatively affected. It's all about *adjusting flow for maximum efficiency*.

Given these considerations about portfolio taxonomy runway, let's proceed with techniques and templates for the more complex organization requiring a fully developed taxonomy.

The templates I'm about to illustrate are intended for use right in the work-item detail of your organization's backlog tool. Your Agile

PMO or Transformation Office may have already set standards and governance for backlog use and taxonomy structure. While this governance is important for monitoring health and outcomes of the organizational system of delivery via consistency and uniformity, many organizational efforts at backlog governance are beginning to show their age as artifacts reinforcing Agile V1.

Additionally, until the tools industry can catch up with more flexible backlog tools suitable for Agile V2, templates can be used to good effect to provide better conversation signal than what TFS, Jira, and Rally can offer, even after heavy customization.

To facilitate monitoring delivery system health, many organizations mandate particular ways in which backlog tools should be used. The templates I'm about to illustrate are in no way meant to replace or subvert your organization's backlog tool governance. If your organization requires administration of entry/exit criteria, risks, and dependencies directly through the standard tool functionality that address these areas, continue doing so. If your organization requires a MoSCow prioritization field to be completed in a work-item detail (even though MoSCoW is not used in this book), continue to do so. See this video for an in-depth explanation of prioritizing work-items.

Let;s remember the theme of this book, which is exploring and enhancing the value of the organizational conversation; all these templates are intended to do is represent frames in the organizational conversation that are specific to particular work-items, given the amount of available signal at the time. They help start, and just as importantly, provide some degree of certainty for when these conversations can be stopped. When applied correctly, templates, used at alignment points, facilitate team effort to increase signal and reduce noise over time, ultimately producing value.

When employed as part of the daily conversation flow, templates can:

- Alleviate the need for complicated process documents.
- Help teams work more efficiently by both simplifying communication load via structure and making remaining communication more high value - ideal for remotely located teams.
- Organize dependency tracking and risk management with structure and flow.
- Encourage moving away from big-bang plans to planning as a daily activity in a simple, consumable, changeable, repeatable, and therefore measurable fashion.
- And what follows, devalue the need for stop-the-world events like program increment (PI) planning – such events are simply too inefficient for remotely operating teams.
- Represent a measurable flow, which makes continuous improvement that much easier to attain.

What follows are templates that are conversation starters to use as a baseline reference. Modify as you see fit, but be sure to understand (*Emulate and Embrace*) what it means to engineer an efficient organizational conversation that increases signal and decreases noise, is repeatable and therefore measurable, and encourages the agile value of continuous improvement (*Establish*).

Template Element Usability in the Backlog Tool

TFS, Rally, and Jira all include a table builder tool in the description and notes sections of their work-item detail editor. Use the table builder tool to create the templates and place in these sections as you see fit. Backlog tools provide general template functionality, so build out all the following elements and save them to a work-item template. Keep in mind it's important that the templates are easily visible to any of the team members working on these items, since these templates serve as both your conversation starters, and determine where in the conversation flow a work-item is. The intended result is more team participation without a dependence on meetings to get anything done. Just open up the detail of a work-item to see exactly where it is in the conversation flow.

The element templates can generally be broken into two groups: Work-item detail sub-conversations, and templates that represent flows of these detail sub-conversations into a single work-item conversation.

Sample Conversation container

Figure 10.1

Enablers (Solutions for Non-Functional Criteria)	In Progress	Done

The work-item sub-conversations are meant to capture signal about work-item specifics in a structured and thorough way.

The flow templates direct the conversation as the signal is captured through multiple statuses. The current status of the work-item conversation flow is updated with the following signoff format:

Initials, start date then once status is completed, add an end date, like so: Initials, Start Date, End Date

Multiple date range entries can be used to specify "**Active**" and "**Hold**" date ranges if flow efficiency calculations are also desired.

Update the flow given which sub-conversation is being held, as seen in the example snippet below:

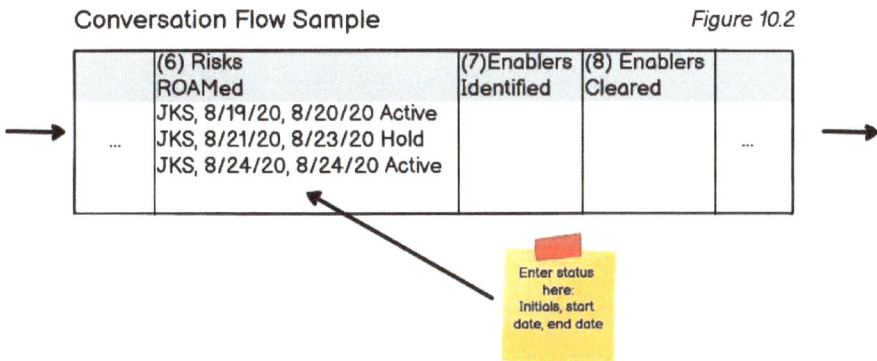

Conversation Flow Sample   *Figure 10.2*

(6) Risks ROAMed JKS, 8/19/20, 8/20/20 Active JKS, 8/21/20, 8/23/20 Hold JKS, 8/24/20, 8/24/20 Active	(7)Enablers Identified	(8) Enablers Cleared	

Enter status here: Initials, start date, end date

Given the examples above, once the conversation about Enablers has begun in *Figure 10.1*, update Status (7) in *Figure 10.2*. After the conversation about Enablers is completed, update Status (8) in *Figure 10.2*. For more on Enablers, see *Figure 12.7* and its following paragraph.

Conversation Flow Working Agreement

Once any status is updated with a final end date, the conversation for that status is considered ended, allowing for conversation for the next flow status to be begin. It should be understood that built into the overall flow is the freedom to completely iterate over it as many times as necessary to meet the work item owner's definition of done.

Starting at the Investment alignment point, let's put the template elements together to see a conversation flow in action.

Coconut Grove, August 27, 2020

CHAPTER 11
INVESTMENT TEMPLATES AND TECHNIQUES

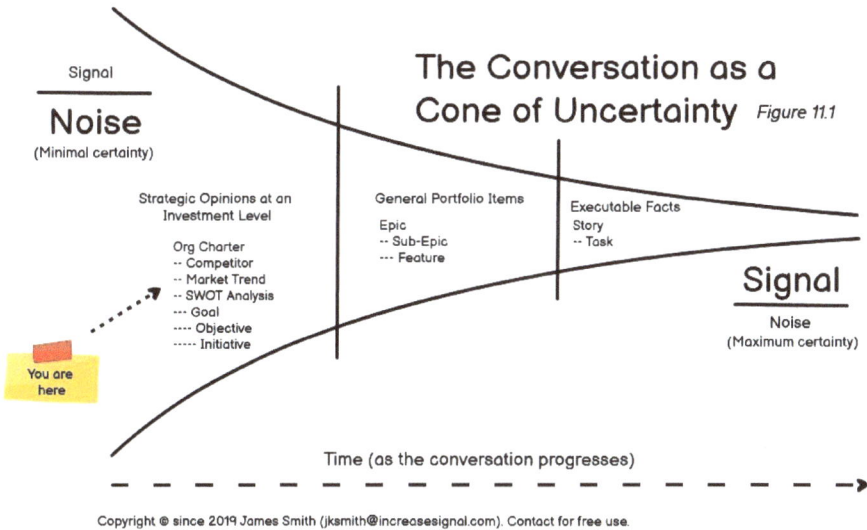

The Conversation as a Cone of Uncertainty *Figure 11.1*

Signal

Noise
(Minimal certainty)

Strategic Opinions at an Investment Level

Org Charter
-- Competitor
-- Market Trend
-- SWOT Analysis
--- Goal
---- Objective
----- Initiative

You are here

General Portfolio Items

Epic
-- Sub-Epic
--- Feature

Executable Facts

Story
-- Task

Signal

Noise
(Maximum certainty)

Time (as the conversation progresses)

In our reference system, we have three general alignment points framing the organizational conversation: The Investment point creates and feeds signal to the Portfolio, and the Portfolio creates and feeds signal to the Delivery teams. The Delivery teams execute on signal from the Portfolio to create organizational value delivered to the customer.

The Investment alignment point represents the beginning of the organizational conversation. Not a lot of signal lives here, since this part of conversation represents the testing ground for assertions, hypotheses, and strategic opinions. It's where we discuss ideas, turn the good ideas into initiatives and toss the bad ones. But it also is the source of truth for the story that the whole organizational taxonomy descends from.

Investment Taxonomy *Figure 11.2*

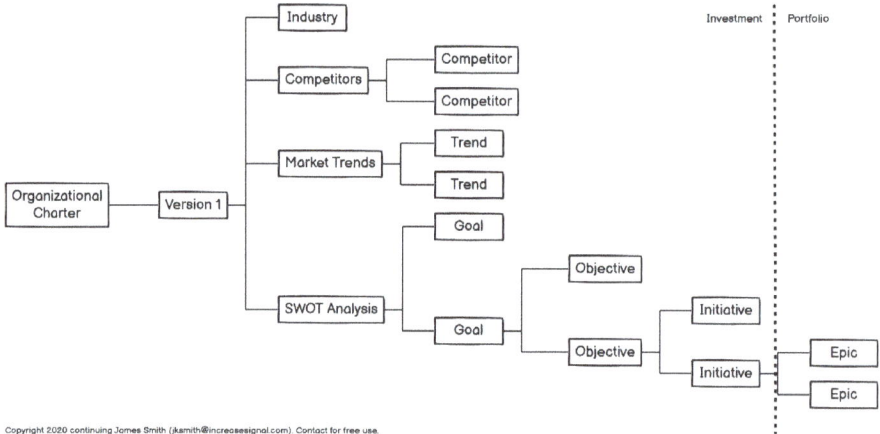

The investment taxonomy is the source of truth maintained by leadership to be delivered to two audiences, external and internal. If the organization is looking for investors or buyers, this is where those groups will spend a lot of time. The organization's employees also need to have a sense of the big picture. The Investment taxonomy is a great place to radiate that information internally.

The organizational charter is the root of the whole taxonomy (*see Figure 11.2*). It's a work-item just like any other in the taxonomy. Use the Organizational Charter work-item to describe the organization's reason for existing, its mission and its vision. As with Versions for any of the Investment work-items, make use of the Version point to provide clear pathways for holdings, divisions, revisions, pivots, acquisitions, and other changes in company size. Whatever is needed to map out the organization's quest for world domination, this taxonomy provides a starting point for the runway to support it.

Child work-items for the Organizational Charter include items dedicated to defining your competitive space. Describe the industry this organization is a part of, identify the organization's competitors, and related market trends.

Finally, given the focus and context the competitive space work-items have provided, a launching point is needed for opinions regarding how to create, correct, enhance, protect, measure, and retire value. A SWOT analysis is a great way to corral these opinions for further go/no-go conversation.

From the SWOT analysis, we may need goals to have enough runway for objectives, or go straight to working on objectives. No need to be gratuitous in our efforts (*see Figure 11.2*). Remember to "maximize the amount of work not done."

Objectives can be constructed as OKR's as desired, and the results more or less map to initiatives. The definition of Initiatives should include both guardrail criteria and value criteria, which will be executed provided the guardrail criteria are met. The following templates can be used as conversations to flesh out Initiative work-item detail:

Figure 11.3

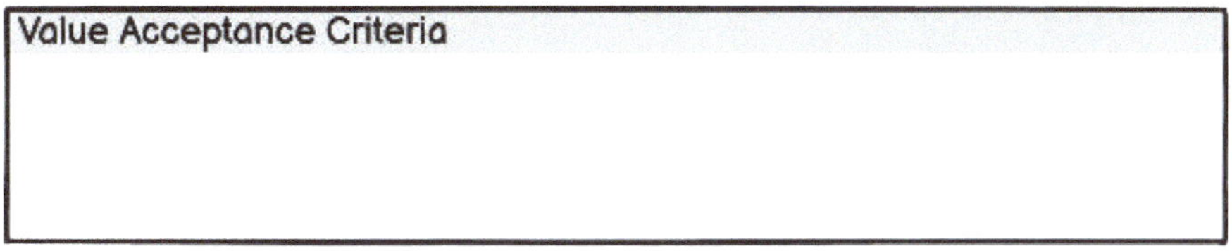

Value Acceptance Criteria

What is the proposed value this Initiative will bring to the organization? Frame that conversation here. If the Initiative is given a "GO" decision, these criteria will more or less each map to Epic items in the portfolio.

Figure 11.4

Guardrail 1: Conversation about Stakeholder Engagement Dependency

The conversation about dependency on stakeholder engagement is the first guardrail conversation. There should be a general understanding of what kind of stakeholder engagement will be required and likely to be received to successfully execute this initiative.

Figure 11.5

Guardrail 2: Conversation about Dependencies on other Initiatives

It's important to have a conversation about dependencies on other initiatives that this initiative might have, since they have their own guardrail dependencies as well, and so on.

Figure 11.6

Guardrail 3: Conversation about Cost

The third guardrail considering cost is valuable since it helps us frame the organization's tolerance for potential cost of this initiative. These *Prospective Costs* estimates shouldn't exist in a vacuum; *Sunk Costs* shouldn't either, unless you want to be strict about your economics.

Consider the backlog as the historical log of a rolling organizational conversation on costs that hasn't been finished yet.

The conversation about costs includes the effort needed to realize this initiative – difficult to quantify at this level without a lot of historical data facilitating relative size estimation. Portfolio team input will be required, provided they have the capacity. If not, consider adding another team at the portfolio level that will act as a proof-of-concept or prototype tiger team. This team should be proficient at doing the research required to assemble a skeleton taxonomy, and collect input from delivery teams to create a minimally viable cost estimate model as quickly as possible.

POC and prototype tiger teams can be of very high value at this level, since they contribute to maturing a key characteristic of a high performance organizational conversation – the ability to continually adjust a lean organizational budget, instead of relying on wasteful legacy annual budgeting techniques. This ability provides a clear competitive advantage that maximizes return on investment and facilitates time to market.

Figure 11.7

Guardrail 4: Conversation about Portfolio Capacity

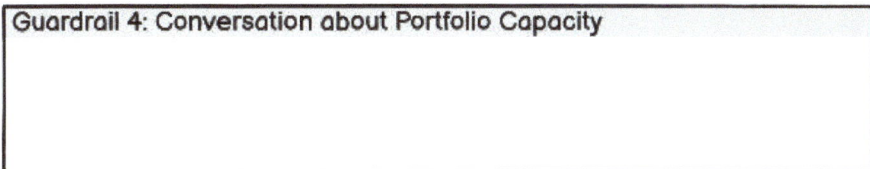

Finally, the fourth guardrail is a conversation about portfolio capacity given all other conclusions about this initiative. Does the responsible portfolio team have enough execution bandwidth at the appropriate time, given the Portfolio inventory? This conversation will of course require collaborative input driven by the Portfolio

Team.

Given these baseline conversational elements, let's see how we can flow the Initiative conversation around them:

Investment Initiative Conversation Flow

Figure 11.8

(1) Owner Appointed	(2) Acceptance Criteria	(3) Stakeholder Engagement	(4) Dependencies on other Initiatives	(5) Cost of Initiative	(6) Portfolio Capacity

(7) Calculate Cost of Barriers	(8) Guardrail Weight	(9) Owner Acceptance	(10) Ready for Portfolio	(11) Cycle Time (S10-S1)+1	(12) Lead Time

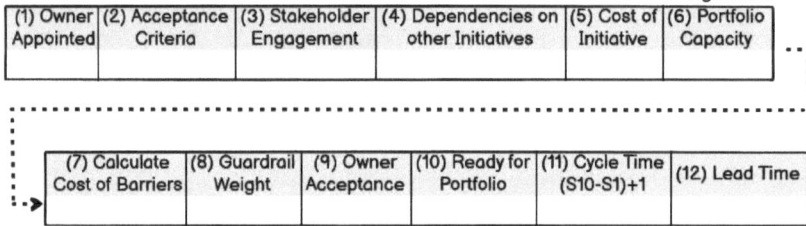

Guardrail Weight Calculation

Stakeholder Engagement Estimation (SE)	Dependencies on Other Initiatives Estimation (DI)	Cost of Initiative Estimation (CI)	Calculate Cost of Barriers: SE+DI+CI	Portfolio Capacity Estimation (PC)	Calculate Guardrail Weight: Cost of Barriers/PC

Description of status flow:

(1) **Owner Appointed**: The conversation about Initiatives starts here. A member of the investment team agrees to take ownership of, and responsibility for this particular Initiative, which includes representation for subject matter expertise. The Initiative Owner (IO) also acts as single source of truth for the investment team working on this initiative. The IO will coordinate with any stakeholders for additional information input, and will ultimately act as **go/no-go** authority for completion of the initiative.

In the spirit of reciprocating the agile value of *trust* and team ownership, the IO role can be filled by anyone on the Investment team, as appropriate. Once a team member accepts the IO role, the member's initials should be entered in this status.

Organizational Working Agreement

> For any work-item at the Investment or Portfolio level, any member of the team can and should be expected to volunteer as the owner of that work-item.

As the (2) acceptance criteria and (3-6) guardrail conversations are completed, their respective statuses are updated in the suggested initials and date fashion described in *Chapter 10.* Additionally, as each guardrail status is updated, a companion complexity score should be entered in the **Guardrail Weight Calculation** table. As with the rest of the organizational conversation, for the sake of uniformity, use points from the Fibonacci scale.

Now the workflow provides an opportunity to calculate the Cost of Barriers:

(7) **Calculate Cost of Barriers**: To calculate, add (SE) Stakeholder Engagement, (DI) Dependencies on other Initiatives, and (CI) Cost of Initiative. The result is a weight that represents the risk of barriers to executing this initiative. The larger the weight, the higher the risk.

Next in the Guardrail Weight calculation, we need a score that represents the **Portfolio Capacity Estimation (PC)**, once the companion conversation has been completed. The lower the score, the lower the portfolio capacity.

(8) **Guardrail Weight**: Cost of Barriers/PC. The higher the score, the higher the execution risk for the initiative. What follows is a high Cost of Barriers can still be tolerated if there is plenty of portfolio capacity, suggesting that the Initiative might still be worth the effort.

Finally, the IO reviews and either accepts or rejects the initiative, as updated in (9) **Owner Acceptance**. If the initiative is rejected, a conversation should be held regarding re-iterating over the initiative or abandoning it.

Initiative Working Agreement for the Portfolio Team

> Portfolio Team members will regularly scan Investment backlog Initiatives with updated "Ready for Portfolio" statuses.

If the IO updates the (10) **Ready for Portfolio** status, then the Initiative is ready to be executed by the Portfolio team.

Finally, calculate the Initiative (11) **Cycle Time** with the given formula.

Exercise Question 5) How would you calculate the Lead Time for this initiative in your head? (***Hint:*** *Read the rest of the book for the answer.*)

Before we see how we can execute an Initiative with a **"GO"** status in the Portfolio, let's take a look at the template elements we can use to capture the conversation at the Portfolio and Delivery alignment points.

Miami Beach, August 20, 2020

CHAPTER 12
PORTFOLIO AND DELIVERY WORK-ITEM CONVERSATION ELEMENTS

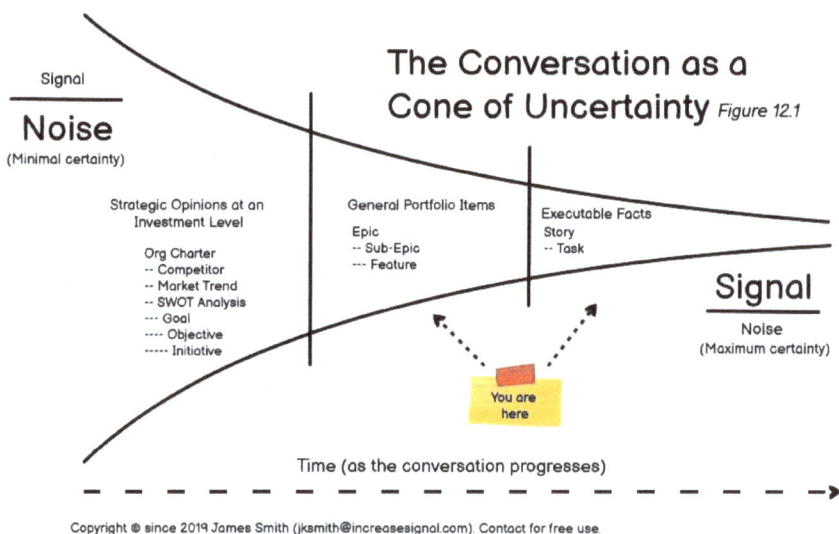

The Conversation as a Cone of Uncertainty *Figure 12.1*

Signal

Noise
(Minimal certainty)

Strategic Opinions at an
Investment Level

Org Charter
-- Competitor
-- Market Trend
-- SWOT Analysis
--- Goal
---- Objective
----- Initiative

General Portfolio Items

Epic
-- Sub-Epic
--- Feature

Executable Facts

Story
-- Task

Signal

Noise
(Maximum certainty)

You are here

Time (as the conversation progresses)

Epic, Sub-Epic, Feature, and Story conversations should cover the following topics at a minimum. Don't fill templates with gratuitous information. Leave blank if appropriate. The point is that the conversation flow was repeated, and sub-conversations were started and stopped on the associated topics. The work-item owner will determine when the conversation can be ended *(see work-item specific flow that follows)*. Design and place these tables in the Description or Notes area of your backlog work-item detail as appropriate.

Work Item Acceptance Criteria
Conversations

Figure 12.2

Acceptance Criteria (Value to be delivered by this work item)	
Functional Criteria (What fulfills business value)	**Non-Functional Criteria** (Design standards, work efforts to deliver value)

Note: Criteria for Epics become Sub-Epics. Criteria for Sub-Epics become Features. Criteria for Features become Stories. Criteria for Stories become Tasks.

Acceptance criteria deliver value for the work-item. Functional criteria provide the work-item with business value. Non-functional criteria enable the functional criteria, and address organizational design or architectural standards.

Conversation on Assumptions

Figure 12.3

Assumptions (What did we take for granted?)

It's important to have a conversation about work-item assumptions, as this supports a good faith effort to follow the scientific method. Assumptions facilitate forming a hypothesis which is ultimately tested by customers and markets. They can be reviewed and revised over time to help adjust delivered functionality for increasing value.

Conversation on Risks   *Figure 12.4*

Risks - Update status with ROAM (Resolved, Owned, Accepted, Mitigated)	In Progress	Done

As good stewards of the organization's effort to produce value, it's important to have a conversation about risks surrounding this work-item. Risks not only affect a work-item's ability to deliver value, but the work-item itself may be creating risks along with value. Once a risk is undergoing thorough analysis by the team, enter a date in the "In Progress" status.

Action items resulting from this conversation, along with their disposition can be radiated in the table above. ROAM'ing the risks helps to provide a standard status for the disposition of any particular risk. Acronym definition:

Resolved: Whatever the team's definition of Resolved is. This could include eliminating, avoiding, or devaluing the risk.

Owned: The team has agreed to provide some resolution for the risk.

Accepted: The team accepted the risk and will not act on it.

Mitigated: Instead of completely resolving the risk, the team has taken action to reduce likelihood or impact of risk.

To have a detailed conversation of each risk, consider using risk *bowties*:

Risk Bowtie   *Figure 12.5*

Sources contributing to Risk	Description of Risk Event	Consequences of Risk

Risk bowties are great for encouraging a thorough and ongoing conversation about risks by the entire team, whether the team is co-located or remote.

Conversation about Dependencies   *Figure 12.6*

Dependency	In Progress with Team	Done

Dependencies are always present in the system of delivery. Any non-trivial organizational effort to produce value in the leanest possible way must address dependencies. Some dependencies can be healthy ones, such as those provided by architectural teams or system integrators. Unhealthy dependencies can be considered as a class of risk to be eliminated or mitigated. Either way, dependencies can cause wait states, so they deserve their own conversation in the work-item development flow. Once a dependency is undergoing thorough analysis by the team, enter a date and the actual team clearing or mitigating the dependency in the "In Progress With Team" status.

Conversation about Enablers

Figure 12.7

Enablers (Solutions for Non-Functional Criteria)	In Progress with Team	Done

Enablers are considered to be healthy dependencies. Along with reducing risk, enablers facilitate unlocking value for the work-item(s) they address, now and in the future. But they can also introduce a wait-state into the flow of work-item development. How to handle this disruption of flow will be explored in *Chapter 12. Templates and Techniques for Epic and Sub-epic Conversation Flow.*

Use the table above to help frame the team's conversation. Once an enabler is undergoing thorough analysis by the team, enter a date and the team implementing the enabler in the "In Progress" status.

Now let's look at a template used at the Portfolio alignment point that takes all these mini-conversations and coordinates them into an overall work-item conversation flow.

Sanibel Island, Florida August 14, 2020

CHAPTER 13
TEMPLATES AND TECHNIQUES FOR EPIC AND SUB-EPIC CONVERSATION FLOW

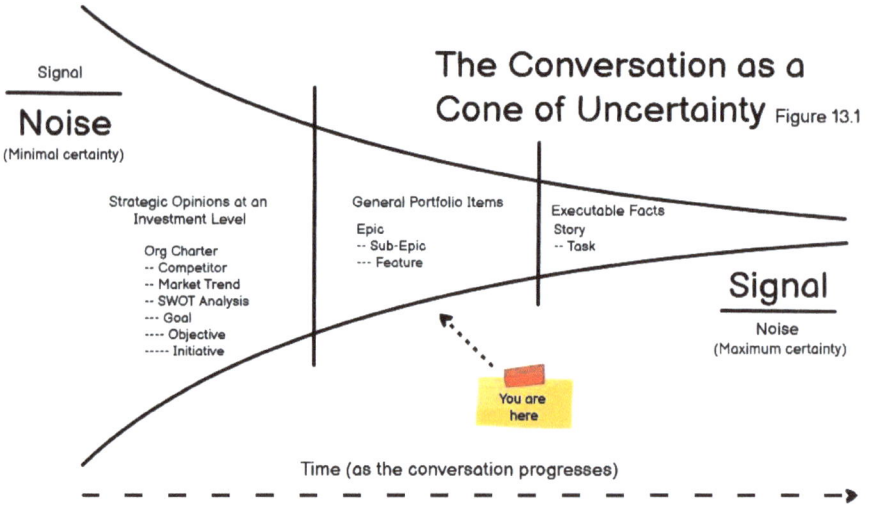

The Conversation as a Cone of Uncertainty Figure 13.1

The following template supports flow for Epics and Sub-Epics. A different template will be used for Features.

Epic and Sub-Epic Conversation Flow

Figure 13.2

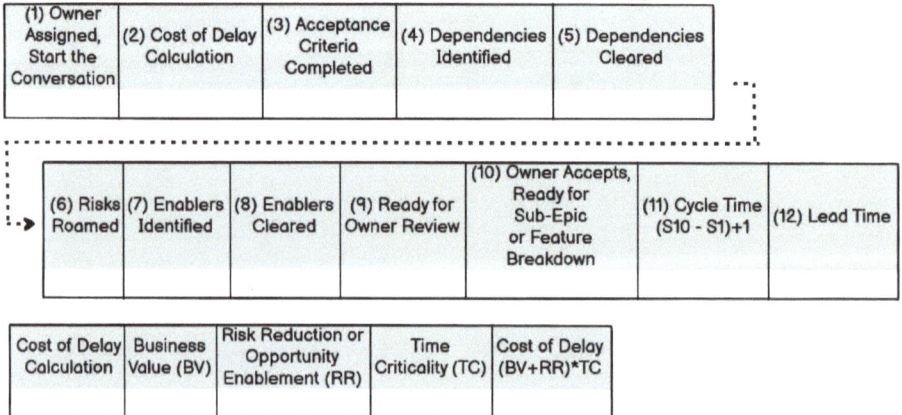

(1) Owner Assigned, Start the Conversation	(2) Cost of Delay Calculation	(3) Acceptance Criteria Completed	(4) Dependencies Identified	(5) Dependencies Cleared	

(6) Risks Roamed	(7) Enablers Identified	(8) Enablers Cleared	(9) Ready for Owner Review	(10) Owner Accepts, Ready for Sub-Epic or Feature Breakdown	(11) Cycle Time (S10 - S1)+1	(12) Lead Time

Cost of Delay Calculation	Business Value (BV)	Risk Reduction or Opportunity Enablement (RR)	Time Criticality (TC)	Cost of Delay (BV+RR)*TC

Status entries are updated as specified in *Chapter 10*. Use this flow to drive the conversation elements explained in *Chapter 12*.

Here are the status entries in the flow explained:

1) **Owner Assigned, Start the Conversation**: Every Epic and Sub-Epic must have a portfolio team member who volunteers as owner. The Epic Owner (EO) and Sub-Epic Owner (SEO) act as subject matter experts for the conversation about this work-item, and also as customer liaison. This helps to keep the overall communication load for the team as lean as possible. Additionally, the (S)EO will act as steward for the conversation, signing off on each status in the flow using the above format.

2) **Cost of Delay Calculation**: Use the template at the bottom of *Figure 13.2* to complete this calculation. Simple story points work well for this calculation, and in the spirit of this qualitative estimation, don't spend a lot of time making the inputs for this calculation perfectly accurate. Cost of Delay is simply used as a prioritization guide. Rely on data collected at the Investment level (see *Chapter 11*) above this Portfolio level to reinforce inputs, and expect these inputs to become more accurate as the delivery system is exercised and produces more historical data.

Additionally, it should be noted that prioritization is actually a combination of prioritization and sequencing, as reflected in a full WSJF (weighted shortest job first) calculation. See *Figure 14.1* for an example of how to do WSJF.

3) **Acceptance Criteria Completed**: Acceptance criteria at the Portfolio alignment point feed the development of sub-work-items. Just as importantly, acceptance criteria drive the requirements of

acceptance tests, and therefore, owner acceptance. Place the table to facilitate this conversation in the work-item description field.

4) **Dependencies Identified**: A conversation about dependencies for this work-item has begun. Use the table in the description of the work-item to facilitate.

Digging into dependency identification often requires a substantial effort. Instead of having confusing yarn parties that cover office walls, it is often just as effective for a team member to volunteer as steward to mitigate or clear a dependency. That steward may reach out to other teams in any alignment point to collect dependency information. If necessary, this effort can be enhanced when the volunteer asks a counterpart on another team to form a dependency pair stewarding effort as needed to complete this part of the work-item conversation. Pairing up to complete tasks is not just for programming.

It's important to note that no dependencies may have been identified for this work-item. That's ok, since there will be other opportunities further into the runway to continue the dependencies conversation. Most importantly though, whether dependencies were found or not, the conversation about dependencies was held by the team in a structured, productive way with a clear starting *and* stopping point.

5) **Dependencies Cleared**: As a result of the dependencies conversation, a signoff of this status will mean that dependencies were either identified then mitigated or eliminated, or no dependencies were identified.

6) **Risks ROAMed**: See *Figure 12.4* and its following paragraph for a

description of the ROAM acronym and how to facilitate the conversation. As with dependencies, the conversation about risks is high-value and held at every level of the conversation taxonomy. Whether risks were identified or not, the conversation about risks was held.

7) **Enablers Identified**: Use the enablers table in the description of the work-item to facilitate this conversation. Enablers can be part of the non-functional criteria in the acceptance criteria conversation for this work-item, or they may be part of the opportunity enablement or risk reduction that this work-item conversation has surfaced.

Enablers could come from suppliers, enabler teams, 3rd party integrators (internal and external) and the like. Because their origin may be outside a particular alignment point's governance, management of enabler development can be a daunting task. But instead of trying to manage this pain point with a complex approach like Large Solution SAFe, first try keeping the management solution simple. Treat this templated flow as if it were a multi-status, multi-flow Kanban board, where the enabler status is essentially a left turn into the enabler provider flow. If the provider is internal, then perhaps you'll have visibility into the provider's workflow. After all, that's one proof that an agile value, transparency, is being met by the organization. If the provider is external, and the relationship with provider is framed by nothing more than contracts and service level agreements, the enabler status becomes a black hole of sorts, but what's important is *time in the black hole is being measured by the system* in a transparent manner. Because of this, historical cycle time measurements will suggest more efficient management of this enabler black hole.

8) **Enablers Cleared**: Meaning enabler solutions have returned from the provider's Kanban or black hole (as the case may be), or no enabler solutions were identified or required. Now the conversation flow can continue.

9) **Ready for Owner Review**: The work-item is now submitted to the work-item's owner for review as a candidate for completion. This is a strategic status in the work-item conversation flow because it is indicative of a highly functioning team over time. Since any team member can volunteer to serve the owner role, this status represents the team managing, planning, and executing their own work – a key characteristic of a lean and competitive system of delivery.

10) **Owner Accepts, Ready for Sub-Epic or Feature Breakdown**: If the owner accepts a work-item which is an Epic, item acceptance criteria are then ready to be mapped to sub-epics. If the item is a Sub-epic, item acceptance criteria are then ready to be mapped to features. If the owner does not accept the item, then it is flowed through the conversation again.

11) **Cycle Time (S10 – S1) + 1**: This calculation reflects the total development time for the work-item. Since there are date ranges in all the statuses in the conversation flow, a cycle time for one or more statuses can be calculated. This type of granular information can be invaluable for pinning down specific wait states in the flow, making it easier to restructure (perhaps using constraint buffers) or regulate flow (using wip limits) to make it more efficient.

12) **Lead Time**: Enter the total time required to deliver the complete epic or sub-epic to the customer. For each epic lead time calculation, all sub-epics will be delivered. For each sub-epic, all features will be

delivered. For each feature, all stories will be delivered. In *Chapter 18*, you'll see a complete flow for the whole organizational conversation that will allow you to track lead and cycle time at every alignment point (and every status) in the conversation.

Huckins Yacht Corporation, Jacksonville, Florida Sep. 1, 2020

CHAPTER 14
CONVERSATION WORKFLOW FOR FEATURES

The Feature conversation is strategic enough that it must have its own chapter. The feature work-item is especially critical to the portfolio taxonomy since it serves as a hand-off point to delivery teams. Additionally, features provide the most data speaking to efficacy of the portfolio runway, as well as solid historicals for data that feed the difficult task of epic effort sizing.

Feature Conversation Flow

Figure 14.1

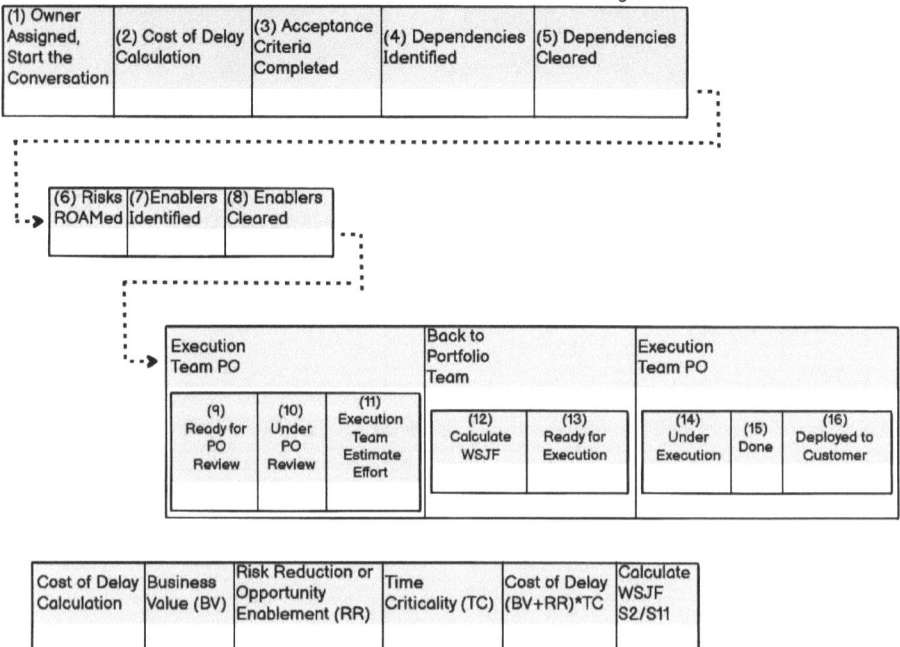

(1) Owner Assigned, Start the Conversation	(2) Cost of Delay Calculation	(3) Acceptance Criteria Completed	(4) Dependencies Identified	(5) Dependencies Cleared

(6) Risks ROAMed	(7) Enablers Identified	(8) Enablers Cleared

Execution Team PO			Back to Portfolio Team		Execution Team PO		
(9) Ready for PO Review	(10) Under PO Review	(11) Execution Team Estimate Effort	(12) Calculate WSJF	(13) Ready for Execution	(14) Under Execution	(15) Done	(16) Deployed to Customer

Cost of Delay Calculation	Business Value (BV)	Risk Reduction or Opportunity Enablement (RR)	Time Criticality (TC)	Cost of Delay (BV+RR)*TC	Calculate WSJF S2/S11

Copyright 2020 continuing James Smith (jksmith@increasesignal.com). Contact for free use

Just as with all other work-item conversations at the portfolio level, before the feature conversation can be started, a team member should volunteer to be owner for this feature. The method for updating each status, and the definition of the first eight statuses is the same as with the Epic/Sub-Epic conversation. All statuses are updated by Feature Owner (FO), unless otherwise noted. Let's define the Feature specific statuses.

(9) **Ready for PO Review**: This status represents the beginning of Delivery Team review of this Feature prior to hand-off to the Delivery Team. The Delivery Team PO will lead this review.

In Kanban terms, this status is actually a constraint buffer. I'll describe the value of this "Ready" status in the working agreements following this flow explanation.

(10) **Under PO Review**: While at the portfolio level the Feature Owner (FO) has stewarded the feature conversation to completion, the Delivery Team still has the go/no-go decision on whether or not it can execute on this feature. The delivery team PO updates this status.

If the team can't execute, it may feel the feature is too large to complete within a reasonable cadence, or the team simply may not understand the feature well enough to be able to execute at all. Either is an indicator that the portfolio runway could be too short, or one or more conversations leading up to hand-off did not generate enough signal to contribute to ultimately producing a feature that could be handed off. If the feature doesn't pass PO review, the PO will update status in standard Initials, Start Date, Stop Date entry fashion, along with the indicator "FAILED." The importance of that status update will be seen later in the Feature Working Agreements.

If the feature does pass initial delivery team review, the PO will update status with standard Initials, Start Date, Stop Date entry, along with "PASSED." As with the "FAILED" status, the importance of that status update will be seen later in the Feature Working Agreements.

The delivery team has one final check and balance for committing to execution of this feature. That's the next status in the flow.

(11) **Delivery Team Estimate Effort**: The delivery team gets a final opportunity to scrutinize a feature by estimating the effort required to complete the feature within a specific cadence (possibly a defined *release window).* It's important that the team use the same units of measurement and scale for effort that was used to calculate Cost of Delay, since it's used in conjunction with Cost of Delay to calculate Weighted Shortest Job First. WSJF is a standard and consistent method for prioritizing work-items which includes both prioritization and sequencing in its calculation.

If the delivery team is unable to estimate effort, then the Feature is essentially rejected by the team, and the conversation will have to be reiterated by the FO. The delivery team PO updates this status with standard update entry, along with the keyword "FAILED."

If the delivery team can estimate the effort for this feature, the delivery team PO updates this status with standard update entry, along with the estimate number.

(12) **Calculate WSJF**: If the delivery team provides an effort estimation, the feature is then handed back over to the FO so that feature WSJF can be calculated. With the resulting score, the FO will either put the feature in a "hold" state or move the feature to the next status.

(13) **Ready for Delivery**: Since this feature now meets the delivery team's Definition of Ready, the portfolio team has completed their conversation for this feature. And if the WSJF conversation results in a score high enough to queue up the feature for delivery, the feature will be moved to this status. When the feature is actually worked on will be determined by the delivery team.

(14) **Under Delivery**: The feature is now under active delivery. This status, along with the following "Done" status are very similar to enabler statuses seen earlier in the conversation flow. The feature now takes a left turn into the delivery team's conversation flow. The delivery team PO updates this status.

(15) **Done**: All stories resulting from the delivery conversation for this feature have met Definition of Done. The delivery team PO updates this status.

(16) **Deployed to Customer**: Whoever has responsibility for releasing to customer is free to update this status. This may be the PO from the delivery team but could also be a PO representative from a dedicated ProdOps team.

Now that the feature has been fully executed and delivered to the customer, our remaining task to complete this feature conversation is to calculate some valuable metrics. The variables in *Figure 14.2* are statuses from the flow:

Feature Conversation Metrics   *Figure 14.2*

Portfolio Cycle Time (S13-S1)+1	Execution Cycle Time (S15-S14)+1	Feature Lead Time (S16-S1)+1

- **Portfolio Cycle Time**: This calculation shows the number of days required to complete the portfolio team's conversation about the feature.
- **Delivery Cycle Time**: This calculation shows the number of days required to complete the delivery team's conversation about the feature.
- **Feature Lead Time**: This calculation shows the number of days required to fully deliver the feature to the customer.

Simply add these results to the results for other features and divide by the total number of features to get average cycle times for a particular calendar interval. Even if your organization collects these values directly from the backlog tool, the value of calculating cycle time and lead time in this fashion can't be underestimated since they encourage familiarity. If we ask our PM's, PO's and teams what their cycle times and lead times are, they'll know instead of replying with the more typical response, "I'd have to run a Jira report." Your teams should know these numbers without having to generate cumulative flow diagrams.

Working Agreements to Support Feature Conversation and Handoff

Since this conversation handles not only feature completion by the portfolio team, but also feature hand-off to the delivery teams, working agreements between the portfolio and the delivery teams act as important guardrails for this hand-off:

Working agreements specific to the **Portfolio Team**:

- Feature owner on Portfolio Team agrees to scan Feature statuses on regular basis, including "PASSED" or "FAILED" statuses recorded in **Under PO Review** status, and either "FAILED" or effort estimation points in **Delivery Team Estimate Effort.**

- If any Feature "Failed" Product PO review or effort estimation, Portfolio Team agrees to reiterate feature conversation until feature either passes delivery team PO review or is de-prioritized in the portfolio.

- Unless done in an agreed to manner, Portfolio Team will not change feature once it is in **Under Delivery** status, as set by Delivery team PO.

- Portfolio Team Feature Owner will update all statuses as they are started/completed in standard format except those statuses specified for Delivery team (PO). FO manages flow.

- Portfolio Team should have at least three features in "Ready for Delivery" status at all times. This is a mandatory WIP that should be regularly adjusted given Cycle Time and Lead Time. (*See Figure 14.2*).

Working agreements specific to the **Delivery Team**:

- Delivery team agrees to deliver updated release plan on a regular basis. This includes recently accepted features. Portfolio team needs this plan to update the Product Roadmap.

- Delivery team PO agrees to scan Portfolio Feature elaboration statuses, specifically **Ready for PO Review**, and **Ready for Delivery**.

- Delivery team PO is responsible for updating Feature conversation statuses:

  - **Under PO Review (PASSED or FAILED)**
  - **Delivery Team Estimate Effort (Points or FAILED)**
  - **Under Delivery**
  - **Done**
  - **Deployed to Customer**
  - **Delivery Cycle Time on the Feature Conversation Metrics template**

If this, or a similar scheme is followed to accomplish hand-off of features for execution, the need for stop-the-world planning sessions involving portfolio and delivery teams is devalued or even eliminated.

Holding costs for parked cruise ships just went way up. Miami Beach, March 25, 2020

CHAPTER 15
AGILE VALUES RECIPROCATION IN THE PORTFOLIO CONVERSATION

Trust, Transparency, Commitment, and Continuous Improvement reciprocated at the Portfolio level

Figure 15.1

Objectives	Evidence
Trust in process	Team owns the conversation flow they execute.
Team members trust each other	Team members share accountability by volunteering to be work item owners.
Trust from Delivery Team	Portfolio conversation flow includes states giving go/no-go decision to Delivery Team for Features. Forced hand-off of features not allowed by process.
Transparency of Process	With exceptions, everyone in organization has at least read-only access into the full organizational backlog, including portfolio backlog, conversation flow, and cycle time calculations for any work item.
Commitment to work item completion	Portfolio team is has right of review and issue of a go/no-go status for strategic initiatives provided by Investment team. If Portfolio team accepts strategic initiative into portfolio conversation flow (go), team commits to completing work.
Continuous Improvement	???

As stated before, the foundation of an effective system of delivery is the cultural contract framed by agile values. To operationalize these agile values, they must be codified right into this delivery system.

Let's take a look at how we did this in the portfolio conversation. The agile values of trust, transparency, and commitment have been codified directly into the portfolio conversation by specifying them as objectives, with mechanisms built into the conversation flow to provide evidence that the objectives have been met.

But the evidence that the continuous improvement objective has been met is missing. Let's examine a couple of ways that evidence can be provided via taxonomy structures.

Taxonomy for Identifying Waste

Figure 15.2

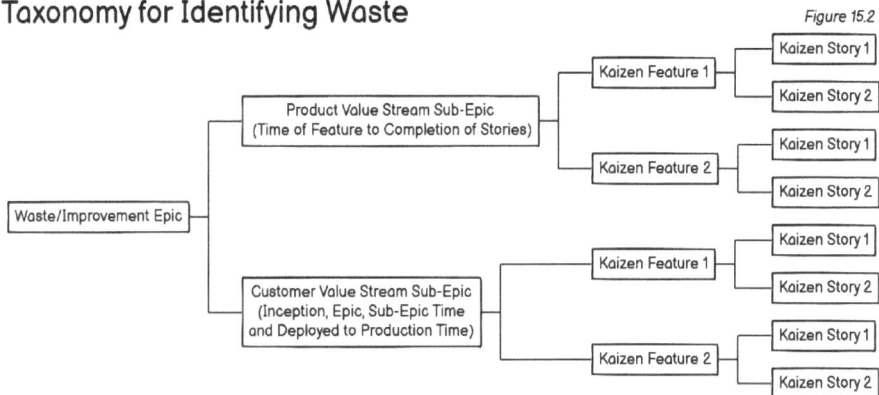

To deliver on the agile value of continuous improvement, we need a method for identifying waste, and treating that waste as a work-item that can be worked through the conversation flow, just like any other work-item. Consider the following taxonomy:

Let's provide some definitions to support this taxonomy:

- Value Stream – system that continuously delivers customer value.

- Value Stream Waste – Any unnecessary effort that delays delivery of value to customer.

- Product Value Stream – the day-to-day activity in your delivery system that produces customer value.

- Customer Value Stream – The part of the stream that is outside of day-to-day activities and intended to deliver customer value. Example: Inception of initiatives, final delivery to customer.

- Kaizen – This is a very important concept contributing to continuous improvement. Kaizen features and stories are the actual improvements meant to identify and mitigate waste in the organizational conversation.

Organizational Working Agreement

> Kaizen features and stories are created by teams to improve their conversations. Since executing on kaizen work items is an activity that is extremely high-value to the organization, teams are free to give high-priority to completion of these work items.

A critical feature of this taxonomy is that portfolio and delivery conversations can execute these work-items just like any delivery work-item. This provides convenient, measurable implementation of improvements in the system of delivery, supported by the cultural contract (specifically, complete transparency). No additional labor or change of process is involved. Indeed, it provides for the improvement taxonomy to *improve itself.*

The taxonomy is designed so that all kaizen stories have a feature parent, just like any other story. Here's a template specific to kaizen feature development:

Kaizen Feature Template

Figure 15.3

Theme and Business Case	

Current State	

Desired State	

Acceptance Criteria (Value to be delivered by this work item)	
Functional Criteria (What fulfills business value)	Non-Functional Criteria (Design standards, work efforts to deliver value)

Be sure to consider changes and additions to any metrics as part of the acceptance criteria.

As with identifying waste, here's an additional taxonomy that provides evidence of continuous improvement:

Strategic Refactoring Taxonomy

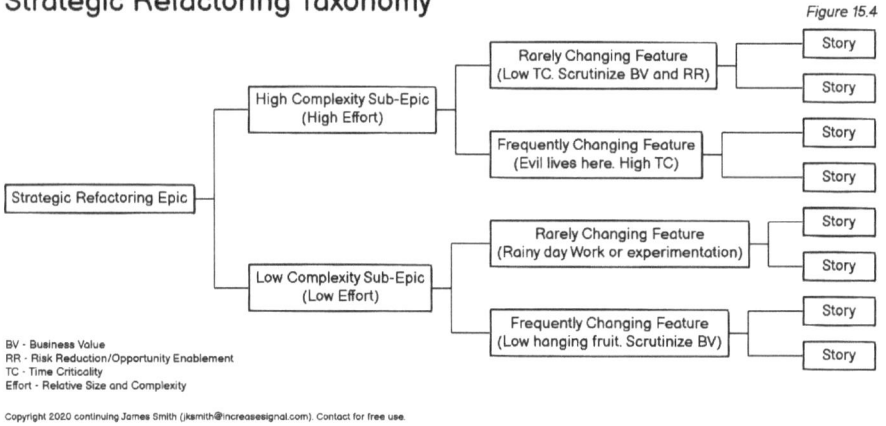

Figure 15.4

BV - Business Value
RR - Risk Reduction/Opportunity Enablement
TC - Time Criticality
Effort - Relative Size and Complexity

Copyright 2020 continuing James Smith (jksmith@increasesignal.com). Contact for free use.

Strategic refactoring is an effort to bring down long-term cost and extend the life of a product. A taxonomy for strategic refactoring provides a means of product improvement that can be executed as part of an overall product taxonomy.

Features can derive from highly complex areas of the product, or areas that could be characterized by low complexity:

Highly complex, rarely changing areas of the product will have a low time criticality, so carefully scrutinize business value and risk reduction for this area.

Highly complex, frequently changing areas of the product have substantive liabilities represented by high time criticality. They should be treated as high priority.

Low complexity, rarely changing areas of the product represent low-priority or experimental work.

Low complexity, frequently changing areas of the product should be prioritized as high, depending on business value. Go ahead and get them done, if possible.

Strategic refactoring is an ongoing activity for any value-producing effort. It can even be used to facilitate refactoring the organizational conversation itself. Note that just as with the Waste Taxonomy, items in the Refactoring Taxonomy can be worked like any other items at Portfolio and Delivery alignment points.

So now we can provide evidence of continuous improvement in the Cultural Contract with the updated reciprocation table:

Trust, Transparency, Commitment, and Continuous Improvement reciprocated at the Portfolio level

Figure 15.5

Objectives	Evidence
Trust in process	Team owns the conversation flow they execute.
Team members trust each other	Team members share accountability by volunteering to be work item owners.
Trust from Delivery Team	Portfolio conversation flow includes states giving go/no-go decision to Delivery Team for Features. Forced hand-off of features not allowed by process.
Transparency of Process	With exceptions, everyone in organization has at least read-only access into the full organizational backlog, including portfolio backlog, conversation flow, and cycle time calculations for any work item.
Commitment to work item completion	Portfolio team is has right of review and issue of a go/no-go status for strategic initiatives provided by Investment team. If Portfolio team accepts strategic initiative into portfolio conversation flow (go), team commits to completing work.
Continuous Improvement	Waste and Refactoring taxonomies to improve conversation and outcomes are executed on a continuing basis.

CHAPTER 16
FLOW TEMPLATE FOR THE DELIVERY CONVERSATION

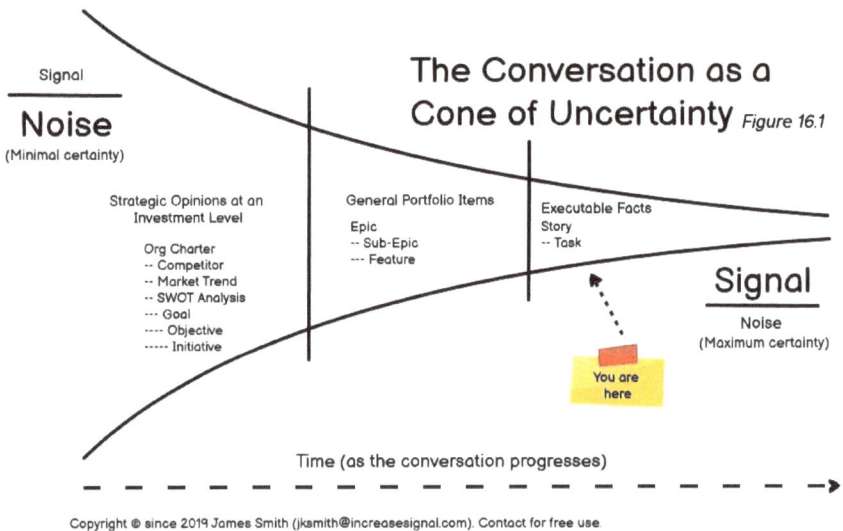

The Conversation as a Cone of Uncertainty *Figure 16.1*

The initial conversation at the delivery alignment point is just as much the ending of the feature handoff conversation as it is the beginning of the delivery conversation. Features still have to be broken down into stories, and to facilitate this, Scrum teams often pull *research stories* into their sprints for delivery. The problem is, Scrum is not designed to deliver these kinds of stories. Scrum is all about consistently delivering increments of customer value on cadence. No matter how we like to spin the notion of what "customer value" is, research stories do not deliver customer value. They are intended to help create stories that deliver customer value.

So does that mean we must pick either Scrum or Kanban at the delivery level? No, what this means is that we continue to practice fundamentals that support an efficient conversation delivering valuable outcomes. It's important not to confuse this as some mixture of Scrum and Kanban, which just brings out the worst of both processes.

So since we don't have executable stories yet, we get to the point where we do have executable stories using Kanban, then to actually deliver the stories, we will pull them into a sprint backlog and use Scrum. This approach will greatly deprecate your need to pull research stories into sprints. Since this work is now done outside of the sprint, how it is planned and tracked by the team will be examined in *Chapter 17*.

Let's see how to implement this approach with the help of a flow template implementing what is essentially a Kanban process. Be sure to track story conversation content using the templates in *Chapter 12. Portfolio and Delivery Work-item Conversation Elements*. Remember, use the table tool to build these templates in the description section of the backlog story detail.

As with the preceding flow templates, statuses are updated using the following nomenclature:

Initials
Start date
End date (once status is completed)

Story Conversation Flow

Figure 16.2

(1) Acceptance Criteria	(2) Dependencies Identified	(3) Dependencies Cleared	(4) Risks ROAMed	(5)Enablers Identified

(6) Enablers Cleared	(7) Ready to Estimate	(8) Estimated	(9)Test Cases and Test Data	(10) Implementation Plan

(11) Team Review	(12) Meets DoR	(13) In Sprint	(14) Delivered to Customer

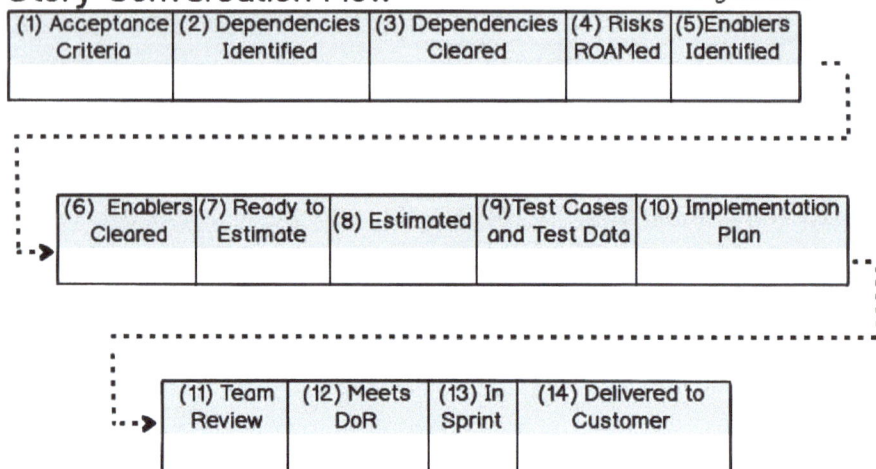

(1) **Acceptance Criteria**: The story product owner is ready for the conversation to begin on this story, so start with the Acceptance Criteria conversation. Until an entry is in this status, no work will be done on the story.

(2) **Dependencies Identified**: Acceptance conversation completed, move on to identifying dependencies, if any.

(3) **Dependencies Cleared**: This status is more restrictive than the same in the conversation flows at the portfolio level. If the delivery team ultimately responsible for executing on this story is a Kanban team, then the dependency could just be managed but still exist. If the delivery is done in a Scrum process, then this status is meant to show that the dependency has been eliminated or is not relevant to story.

(4) **Risks ROAMed**: The conversation about ROAMing risks is covered in _Chapter 12_. Be sure to make use of risk bowties to distill the risk conversation.

(5) **Enablers Identified**: Just as with portfolio work-items, enablers provide some capability, often identified via the conversation regarding non-functional acceptance criteria.

(6) **Enablers Cleared**: Enabler conversation has taken place, and story conversation can continue to the next status.

(7) **Ready to Estimate**: This status helps remind Product Owners that the effort for this story is ready to be estimated during the backlog refinement activity that happens during the sprint.

(8) **Estimated**: Once the responsible delivery team has estimated this story, this status is updated with estimation points and standard initials/dates entry.

(9) **Test Cases and Test Data**: Especially if the delivery team is using Scrum, test cases and test data should be gathered in advance of story delivery. This avoids wait states (or even worse, external dependencies) that might occur during the sprint. Additionally, it's important for the PO to have a conversation regarding tests to run up front. The PO should provide steps on what tests this story should pass in order to meet Definition of Done. That will make general sprint development time and acceptance test review that much more efficient.

(10) **Implementation Plan**: if necessary, for clarity and moving this story to meeting Definition of Ready, the delivery team is free to do some degree of an implementation (tasking) plan for this story. The remainder of the plan can always be completed in sprint planning for a Scrum team.

(11) **Team Review**: The story conversation is now ready for review by the team. It is the responsibility of each team member to update this status with initials and date. If full consensus of team is met, the story conversation is ended as it has met team Definition of Ready.

(12) **Meets DoR**: Story has met delivery team's Definition of Ready, and PO has determined that this story should be considered as a candidate for including in a near term sprint.

Exercise Question 6) Why do dependencies have to be eliminated in the Scrum process, but not in Kanban?

(13) **In Sprint**: The story is in progress for completion in a sprint, as reflected by sprint start date and PO initials.

(14) **Delivered to Customer**: Once the PO signs off on this status, and the same status for all other stories belonging to the same parent feature, lead time for parent feature can be calculated.

Organizational Working Agreement

Once all **stories** or equivalent work items are delivered to the customer, the lead time for their parent **feature** should be updated. Once all **features** or equivalent work items are delivered to the customer, the lead time for their parent **sub-epic** should be updated. Once all **sub-epics** or equivalent work items are delivered to the customer, the lead time for their parent **epic** should be updated. Once all **epics** or equivalent work items are delivered to the customer, the lead time for their parent **investment initiative** should be updated.

Redington Beach, August 15, 2020

CHAPTER 17
CEREMONY TEMPLATES FOR HIGH PERFORMANCE SCRUM TEAMS

It's understood that if the delivery team uses the Kanban process, delivery within a certain time period is less certain, but Kanban may simply be the best choice, given its flexibility. But if the work is suitable for Scrum (which is the intent of the story conversation described in *Chapter 16*) then let's take a look at how high-performing Scrum teams conduct their ceremonies to facilitate delivery certainty on cadence. Each template radiates a wealth of information that reciprocates the agile value of *transparency*.

Sprint Planning

Figure 17.1

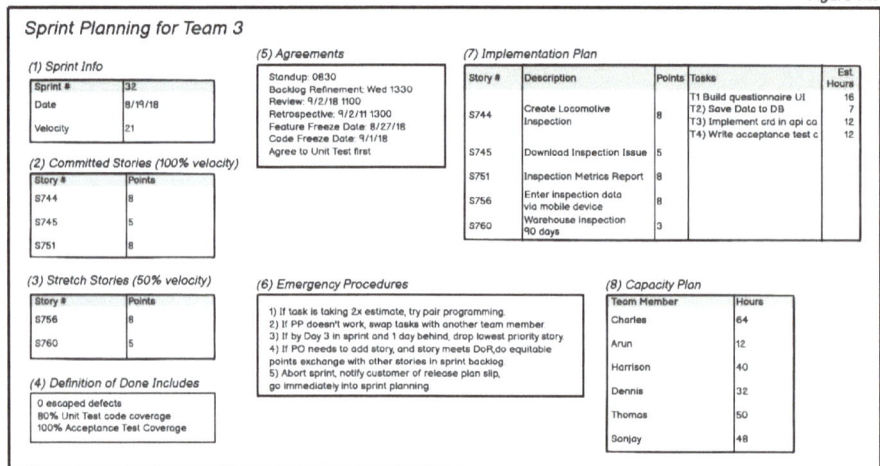

Sprint Planning for Team 3

(1) Sprint Info

Sprint #	32
Date	8/19/18
Velocity	21

(2) Committed Stories (100% velocity)

Story #	Points
S744	8
S745	5
S751	8

(3) Stretch Stories (50% velocity)

Story #	Points
S756	8
S760	5

(4) Definition of Done Includes

0 escaped defects
80% Unit Test code coverage
100% Acceptance Test Coverage

(5) Agreements

Standup: 0830
Backlog Refinement: Wed 1330
Review: 9/2/18 1100
Retrospective: 9/2/11 1300
Feature Freeze Date: 8/27/18
Code Freeze Date: 9/1/18
Agree to Unit Test first

(6) Emergency Procedures

1) If task is taking 2x estimate, try pair programming.
2) If PP doesn't work, swap tasks with another team member.
3) If by Day 3 in sprint and 1 day behind, drop lowest priority story.
4) If PO needs to add story, and story meets DoR, do equitable points exchange with other stories in sprint backlog.
5) Abort sprint, notify customer of release plan slip, go immediately into sprint planning.

(7) Implementation Plan

Story #	Description	Points	Tasks	Est. Hours
S744	Create Locomotive Inspection	8	T1 Build questionnaire UI	16
			T2) Save Data to DB	7
			T3) Implement crd in api ca	12
			T4) Write acceptance test c	12
S745	Download Inspection Issue	5		
S751	Inspection Metrics Report	8		
S756	Enter inspection data via mobile device	8		
S760	Warehouse Inspection 90 days	3		

(8) Capacity Plan

Team Member	Hours
Charles	64
Arun	12
Harrison	40
Dennis	32
Thomas	50
Sanjay	48

Let's start with a sprint planning template that can be set up in tools such as SharePoint or Confluence:

What's important about this ceremony as with the other ceremonies, is that it be repeated the same way and include the same elements every time the ceremony is conducted. Anything repeated can be measured for effectiveness, giving the team a better opportunity to reciprocate the agile value of continuous improvement via their ceremonies.

So let's start from the top and move down and to the right through the template flow.

(1) Sprint Info   Figure 17.2

Sprint #	32
Date	8/19/18
Velocity	21

Always start planning with Sprint Info that includes the current sprint id, start date of sprint, and expected velocity for this sprint. Your best indicator of expected velocity will generally be the velocity of the team's last sprint.

Exercise Question 7) Why should expected velocity generally be driven by velocity of the team's last sprint instead of an average of prior sprints?

(2) Committed Stories (100% velocity)   Figure 17.3

Story #	Points
S744	8
S745	5
S751	8

These are the prioritized stories the PO is asking the team to commit to the sprint backlog. Note that they generally add up to expected velocity. This element of the sprint planning template reciprocates the agile value of *commitment,* since the team will review these stories to determine confidence that they can be completed. The team will only commit if confidence is high.

(3) Stretch Stories (50% velocity)   Figure 17.4

Story #	Points
S756	8
S760	5

If the team completes their committed stories, they are free to pull in these prioritized stretch stories as designated by the PO. We will see later in the Sprint Review template why the PO will typically bring 150% of the team's velocity to sprint planning for consideration. Stretch stories must meet the team's **Definition of Ready** to be considered. Note that since these stories meet **DoR,** they cannot be changed by the PO, whether they are completed in the sprint or not.

In combination with capacity planning, this element of sprint planning represents the team's structured approach to reciprocating *continuous improvement.*

(4) Definition of Done Includes   Figure 17.5

0 escaped defects
80% Unit Test code coverage
100% Acceptance Test Coverage

The technical portion of the Definition of Done should be reviewed at every sprint planning. This element of sprint planning is the reciprocation of the team's *commitment* to *continuous improvement* to the product they are delivering. *Trust* given by the PO to meet Definition of Done is also reciprocated in this element, since the team has agreed to 100% acceptance test coverage. Even if this area never changes, for the benefit of repeatable process it should always be reviewed.

(5) Agreements   **Figure 17.6**

```
Standup: 0830
Backlog Refinement: Wed 1330
Review: 9/2/18 1100
Retrospective: 9/2/11 1300
Feature Freeze Date: 8/27/18
Code Freeze Date: 9/1/18
Agree to Unit Test first
```

Team agreements should be reviewed, modified as necessary, and agreed to at every sprint planning as well. This act reciprocates acknowledgment and *commitment to the sprint itself* by the team.

(6) Emergency Procedures   **Figure 17.7**

```
1) If task is taking 2x estimate, try pair programming.
2) If PP doesn't work, swap tasks with another team member.
3) If by Day 3 in sprint and 1 day behind, drop lowest priority story.
4) If PO needs to add story, and story meets DoR, do equitable
points exchange with other stories in sprint backlog.
5) Abort sprint, notify customer of release plan slip,
go immediately into sprint planning.
```

Since a Scrum team is meant to be the most dependable alignment point to execute against the portfolio in the organizational conversation, sprint commitments are taken very seriously. That's why the Scrum team makes use of Emergency Procedures. Pre-defined emergency procedures as determined by the team are handy because they help the team avoid trying to figure out what to do in the middle of a sprint going awry. Emergency procedures are also reviewed, modified if necessary, and agreed to at every sprint planning. This example serves as a starting point for the emergency procedure conversation.

This element of sprint planning reciprocates the agile values *trust, transparency,* and *commitment.* It reciprocates *continuous improvement* as well, since emergency procedures are reviewed for efficacy at every sprint retro ceremony.

(7) Implementation Plan   *Figure 17.8*

Story #	Description	Points	Tasks	Est. Hours
S744	Create Locomotive Inspection	8	T1 Build questionnaire UI	16
			T2) Save Data to DB	7
			T3) Implement crd in api ca	12
			T4) Write acceptance test c	12
S745	Download Inspection Issue	5		
S751	Inspection Metrics Report	8		
S756	Enter inspection data via mobile device	8		
S760	Warehouse inspection 90 days	3		

If deemed necessary, Scrum teams are free to build out implementation (tasking) plans for each story. Used in conjunction with capacity plans (introduced next), implementation plans represent the final approval checkpoint the Scrum team uses to accept or reject a story into the backlog for the upcoming sprint.

(8) Capacity Plan	Figure 17.9
Team Member	**Hours**
Charles	64
Arun	12
Harrison	40
Dennis	32
Thomas	50
Sanjay	48

The capacity plan represents the hours team members have available to dedicate to the sprint iteration. Along with the implementation plan, the capacity plan represents the only conversation in Scrum that originate estimates based on hours.

If the implementation plan exceeds the capacity plan by more than 130%, the Scrum team should give consideration to rejecting the lowest priority story the PO has brought to sprint planning.

If the capacity plan exceeds the implementation plan by more than 130%, the team can task out an additional stretch story to consider it for inclusion into the (committed) sprint backlog.

This exercise of comparing implementation plan and capacity plan is the final opportunity for Scrum teams to accept or reject stories for inclusion into the upcoming sprint.

In addition, teams should employ an hours-based burn-down chart to help them validate their implementation plans, but also as a health gauge for the sprint that helps them determine when emergency procedures should be activated. Sprint burn-down charts are the sole property of the Scrum team and are not to be considered outside the sprint.

Exercise Question 8) Why should sprint burn-down charts be measured in task hours instead of story points?

The implementation plan and capacity plan work together to reciprocate the agile values of *trust, commitment, and continuous improvement.* Evidence of engaging in this exercise shows that the team is providing highest confidence that it can commit to story completion.

Besides considering capacity for commitment in the upcoming sprint, the capacity plan also helps team members gauge their availability for story refinement leading to Definition of Ready *(see Figure 16.2)*, since this work is completed outside of committed sprint time. For example, if Sanjay *(see Figure 17.9)* has 48 hours available to meet sprint commitments, then he may be planning to spend another 16 hours assisting the PO with refinement conversation flow *(see Figure 16.2)* regarding various stories in the delivery backlog. Another column could certainly be added to this table to indicate those 16 hours, but that's not in the spirit of Scrum and is just extraneous time-tracking. The capacity plan is meant to help the team internally gauge their ability to commit to the delivery of value in the current sprint. Anything outside of that is technically not a commitment by Scrum standards.

A great operational advantage of Scrum is its simplicity; despite any other metrics Jira has available, only a single question needs to be asked of a Scrum team: "Is their velocity trending up?" If the areas in the planning template are followed diligently, everything else about the team, including delivering quality value for the organization, and providing evidence that the cultural contract has been met will follow this velocity trend.

To test the veracity of this notion, create a kaizen story for one of the improvement taxonomies in _Chapter 15_. For Scrum teams, you may find that metrics additional to velocity, such as cycle time (1 iteration) and percentage of stories completed (100%) are inefficient considerations in the organizational conversation.

Scrum Master Tip: First understand why Scrum is supposed to always have a cycle time of one iteration and flow efficiency of 100%. Then, if a team is rolling stories, drop velocity until team reports a cycle time of one iteration and flow efficiency of 100% (in simplest terms, completing all stories committed to during an iteration). Another reason to drop velocity is to help team meet their own quality Definition of Done by allowing zero escaped defects. Then make judicious use of stretch stories (_see Figure 17.4_) to help the team bump up their velocity at an appropriate pace. As a past mentor of mine would always say, "**Slow down to speed up!**"

Sprint Review

Now, let's examine a template for Sprint Review.

Figure 17.10

Sprint Review for Team 3

(1) Sprint Info

Sprint #	32
Date	9/2/18
New Velocity	29

(2) Stories Completed

Story #	Description	Points
S744	Create Locomotive Inspection	8
S745	Download Inspection	5
S751	Inspection Metrics Report	8
S756	Enter Inspection Data via Mobile Device	8

(3) Updated Release Plan

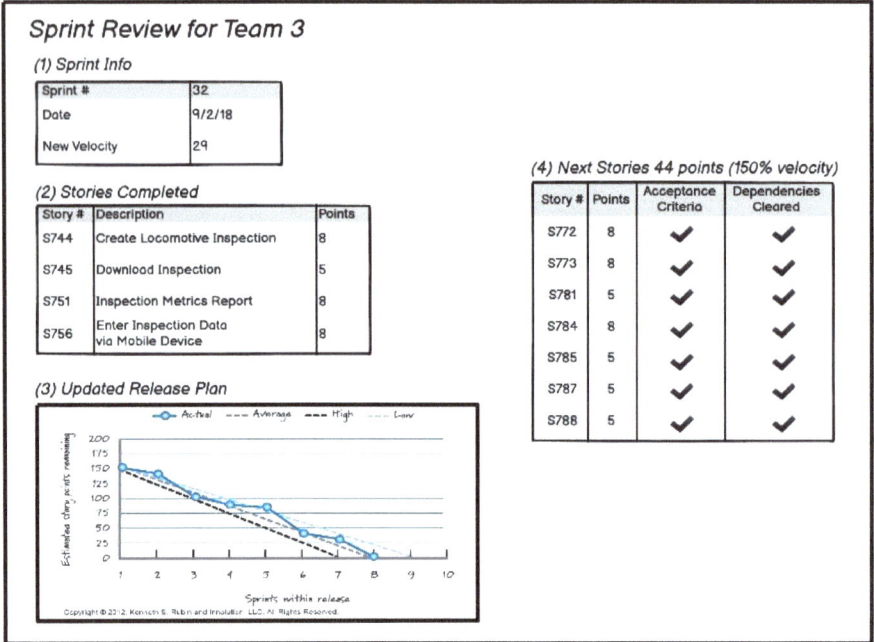
Copyright © 2012 Kenneth S. Rubin and Innolution LLC. All Rights Reserved.

(4) Next Stories 44 points (150% velocity)

Story #	Points	Acceptance Criteria	Dependencies Cleared
S772	8	✓	✓
S773	8	✓	✓
S781	5	✓	✓
S784	8	✓	✓
S785	5	✓	✓
S787	5	✓	✓
S788	5	✓	✓

The sprint review provides an opportunity for the Scrum team to present to stakeholders what it has accomplished during the iteration. As with the planning template, it's important to hold the review conversation the same way every time, since that provides opportunity for inspection and improvement of this ceremony. As with the sprint planning template, create in SharePoint or Confluence to reciprocate the agile value of *transparency*.

(1) Sprint Info
Figure 17.11

Sprint #	32
Date	9/2/18
New Velocity	29

As with the planning template, always start out with sprint number, but note date is the sprint review date agreed to in sprint planning. Also, the team was able to pull in an additional stretch story that has increased their velocity.

(2) Stories Completed — *Figure 17.12*

Story #	Description	Points
S744	Create Locomotive Inspection	8
S745	Download Inspection	5
S751	Inspection Metrics Report	8
S756	Enter Inspection Data via Mobile Device	8

Be sure to list the stories completed by the team, since these stories will be what the team demos to the stakeholders. Since the team has agree to 100% acceptance test coverage and the team worked with the PO to determine what the tests should cover, the team will demonstrate the stories by taking the PO through the tests. After demonstration of each story, the PO will tell the team if that story meets the Definition of Done for business value.

Organizational Working Agreement

Whether for Scrum or Kanban processes, if the team schedules a demo, the whole organization is invited.

This element and the accompanying demo represent some of the best examples of the reciprocation of *trust* and *commitment* in the organizational conversation. The more the team delivers on what they commit to delivering, the more the PO will trust them, and the more the organization will consider the team to be an asset that can reliably deliver the portfolio.

(3) Updated Release Plan   Figure 17.13

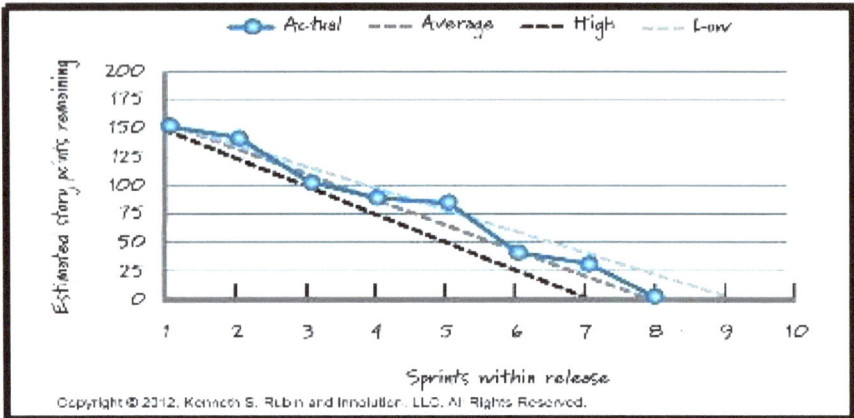

After all stories have been demonstrated, it's now time for the Delivery team to update their release plan. This is important for stakeholders and the Portfolio team, since the Portfolio team is responsible for the Product Roadmap, which they will update given the Delivery team's new release plan.

The team's release plan reciprocates the agile value of *continuous improvement.* As the release burndown chart reveals, if the team is able to get ahead of schedule, that's a *result* of continuous improvement. If the team is falling behind, that's an *opportunity* for continuous improvement, which is how a high-performing team sees failure.

(4) Next Stories 44 points
(150% velocity)

Figure 17.14

Story #	Points	Acceptance Criteria	Dependencies Cleared
S772	8	✔	✔
S773	8	✔	✔
S781	5	✔	✔
S784	8	✔	✔
S785	5	✔	✔
S787	5	✔	✔
S788	5	✔	✔

Executing on the Product Roadmap by Scrum teams can viewed as a *flow of sprints* over time. It's the responsibility of the PO to minimize wait states for the sake of maintaining and enhancing that flow.

So by the time the Scrum team holds a sprint review, the PO has already assembled some high-priority stories equaling 150% of the team's new velocity. While a more thorough review of these sprint candidate stories will be done at the next sprint planning session, to save time, the PO and team can have a pre-review conversation covering the team's basic Definition of Ready requirements. That includes that these stories should at least have completed acceptance criteria and all external dependencies cleared. Scrum execution certainty would be jeopardized if stories with external dependencies are allowed into the sprint, since that means that the team has accepted a story into the sprint which may require work outside of their control. That introduces a wait state into the process they can't address, and more importantly, increases chances that a team could fail in meeting its sprint commitments.

A quick conversation about story candidates for the next sprint in sprint review serves the agile mantra of "just enough, just in time" and so saves time in the upcoming sprint planning. And since the PO brings 150% of the team's new velocity to the conversation, this also reciprocates the agile value of *continuous improvement*, by always providing the opportunity for the Scrum team to bump up their velocity via stretch stories.

Sprint Retrospective

Finally, let's take a look at Sprint Retrospective. The Sprint Retro is supported by a simple template, that as with the preceding templates, reinforces repetition, making it more suitable for inspection and improvement over time. As with the sprint planning and review templates, create in SharePoint or Confluence to reciprocate the agile value of **transparency.**

Figure 17.15

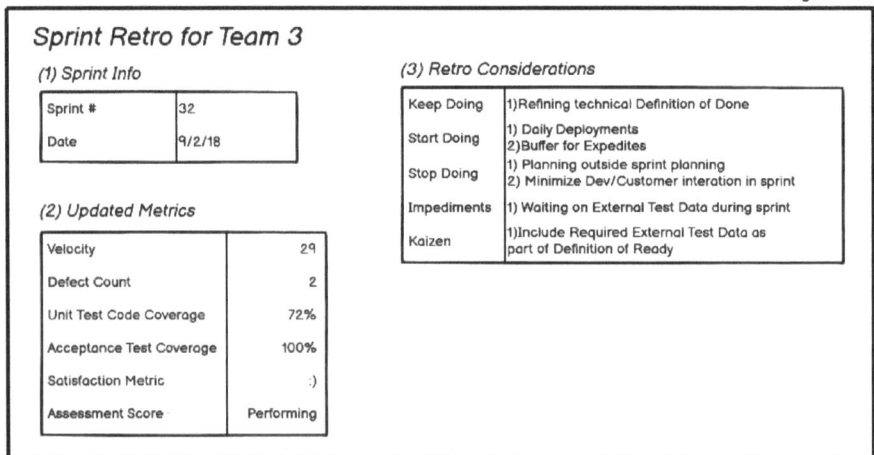

Sprint Retros serve as an inspect and adapt event for the sprint. They should be kept simple, and highly interactive from the start. Taken together, the elements of this template reciprocate all the agile values *of trust, transparency, commitment, and continuous improvement.*

(1) Sprint Info   **Figure 17.16**

Sprint #	32
Date	9/2/18

As with the previous ceremony templates, always start out with sprint number, but note that the date is the sprint retro date agreed to in sprint planning.

(2) Updated Metrics   **Figure 17.17**

Velocity	29
Defect Count	2
Unit Test Code Coverage	72%
Acceptance Test Coverage	100%
Satisfaction Metric	:)
Assessment Score	Performing

Since the Sprint Retro is an inspect and adapt event, it's a great opportunity to review sprint metrics. The first four example metrics above are of particularly high value, since they contribute greatly to quality, and can be derived from simple "mental math" arithmetic. We can always become SME's at how Rally calculates SDPI for instance, but how much more dysfunction do they reveal than the basic calculations above? What I always say perhaps has no better example: "Don't add complexity unless that complexity is worth the dysfunction it addresses." Use any available metrics as necessary, but make sure the basic metrics are used and understood first.

The remaining measurements can be very organization specific. Some organizations are fine with a stock Scrum team Satisfaction Survey downloaded from the web. Other organizations want a very customized means for determining this metric. This metric is very important for the organization; it is almost guaranteed to ultimately affect a team's velocity negatively.

The same goes for assessments. Use of assessments is often misunderstood, so assessments can be subject to heavy customization by the agile organization. Transparency and assessment effectiveness can suffer as a result. Assessments, and how to create and use them will be the subject of a future companion addendum for this book.

If this element of the Sprint Retro is used in the spirit as intended, it provides tracking data for the team that reciprocates the agile value of *continuous improvement*, both in terms of opportunities for, and results of the team's performance.

(3) Retro Considerations

Figure 17.18

Keep Doing	1)Refining technical Definition of Done
Start Doing	1) Daily Deployments 2)Buffer for Expedites
Stop Doing	1) Planning outside sprint planning 2) Minimize Dev/Customer interation in sprint
Impediments	1) Waiting on External Test Data during sprint
Kaizen	1)Include Required External Test Data as part of Definition of Ready

"**Keeps, Starts, and Stops**" represent the classic conversation of the Sprint Retro, and require full participation by the team. Leave the questions general as stated so that anything can be discussed, from process improvement to team internal business.

Also have a discussion around impediments that occurred during the sprint, and how to address them so they don't happen again. Kaizen stories are a great way to deal with sprint impediments and can be included in the Waste or Strategic Refactoring taxonomies as discussed in *Chapter 15*.

When the team produces Kaizen stories, since they are meant to improve the delivery system, the PO should consider them of high importance. They are so important in fact that when the team wants to pull them into a sprint, they are highest priority, and the PO should prioritize additional stories accordingly.

Organizational Working Agreement

> Kaizen features and stories are created by teams to improve their conversations. Since executing on kaizen work items is an activity that is extremely high-value to the organization, teams are free to give high-priority to completion of these work items.

More than any other aspect of Scrum, the team conversation around Keeps, Starts and Stops, Impediments, and Kaizen stories represents the reciprocation of the agile values of *continuous improvement* and *commitment* to that improvement.

At this point, we've filled in the organizational conversation, from the Investment alignment point, to Portfolio, to the Delivery alignment point. Let's put all this together and see what we have.

CHAPTER 18
THE ORGANIZATIONAL CONVERSATION

Let's take a look at the flow of our organizational conversation, from strategic initiative to executable fact and ready for customer delivery:

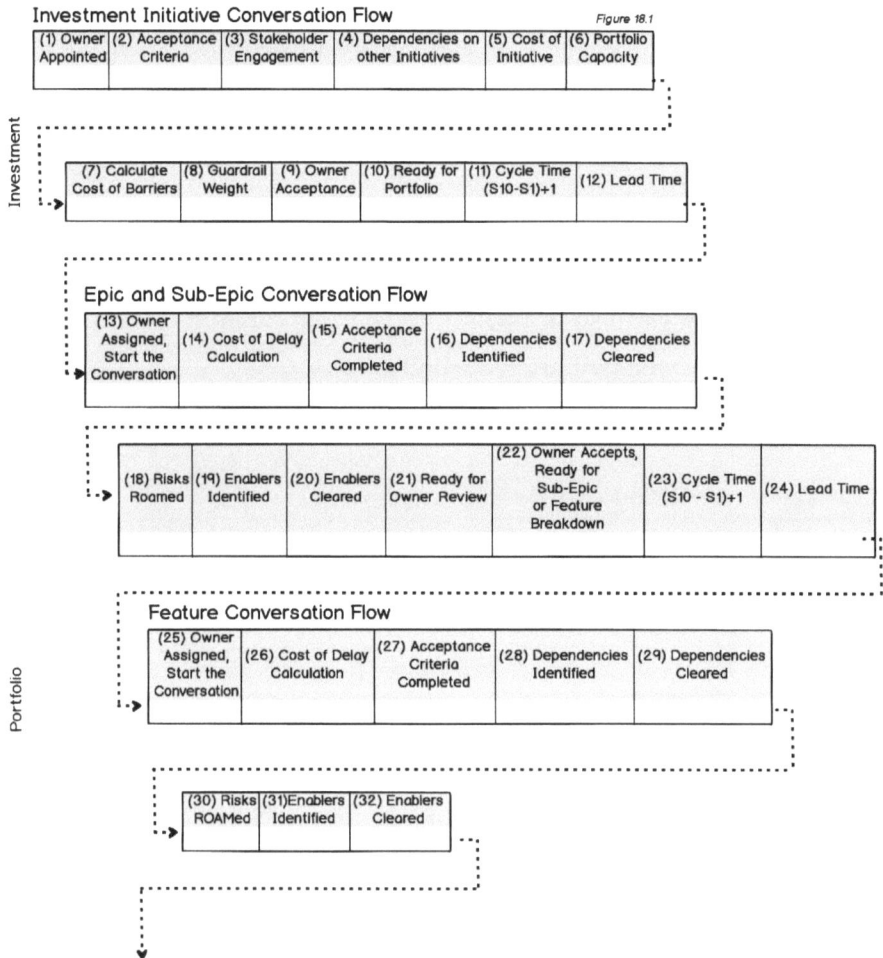

Investment Initiative Conversation Flow — *Figure 18.1*

(1) Owner Appointed	(2) Acceptance Criteria	(3) Stakeholder Engagement	(4) Dependencies on other Initiatives	(5) Cost of Initiative	(6) Portfolio Capacity

(7) Calculate Cost of Barriers	(8) Guardrail Weight	(9) Owner Acceptance	(10) Ready for Portfolio	(11) Cycle Time (S10-S1)+1	(12) Lead Time

Epic and Sub-Epic Conversation Flow

(13) Owner Assigned, Start the Conversation	(14) Cost of Delay Calculation	(15) Acceptance Criteria Completed	(16) Dependencies Identified	(17) Dependencies Cleared

(18) Risks Roamed	(19) Enablers Identified	(20) Enablers Cleared	(21) Ready for Owner Review	(22) Owner Accepts, Ready for Sub-Epic or Feature Breakdown	(23) Cycle Time (S10 - S1)+1	(24) Lead Time

Feature Conversation Flow

(25) Owner Assigned, Start the Conversation	(26) Cost of Delay Calculation	(27) Acceptance Criteria Completed	(28) Dependencies Identified	(29) Dependencies Cleared

(30) Risks ROAMed	(31) Enablers Identified	(32) Enablers Cleared

Investment — *Portfolio*

Delivery

Execution Team PO			Back to Portfolio Team		Execution Team PO		
(33) Ready for PO Review	(34) Under PO Review	(35) Execution Team Estimate Effort	(36) Calculate WSJF	(37) Ready for Execution	(38) Under Execution	(39) Done	(40) Deployed to Customer

(41) Acceptance Criteria	(42) Dependencies Identified	(43) Dependencies Cleared	(44) Risks ROAMed	(45)Enablers Identified

(46) Enablers Cleared	(47) Ready to Estimate	(48) Estimated	(49)Test Cases and Test Data

(50) Implementation Plan	(51) Team Review	(52) Meets DoR	(53) In Sprint	(54) Delivered to Customer

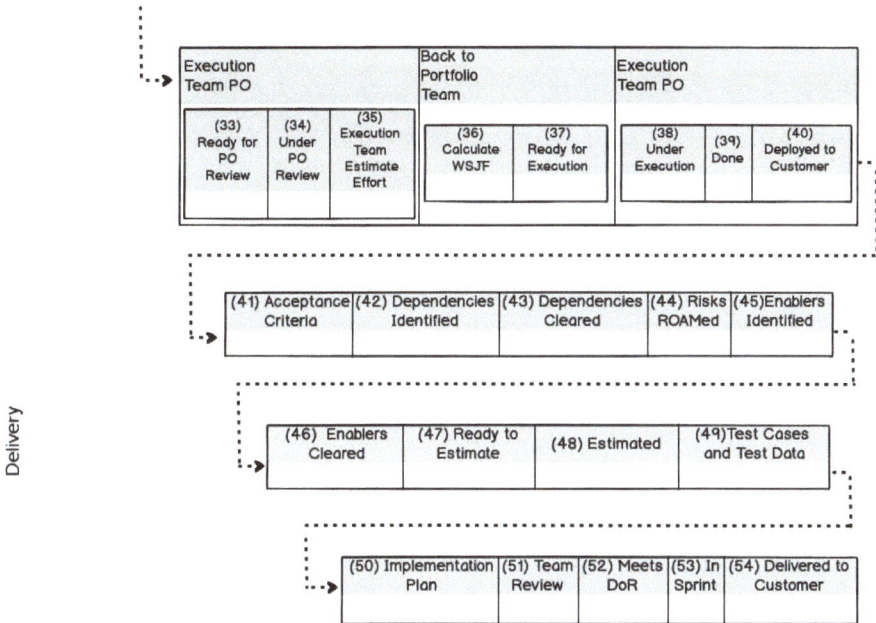

This flow represents a conversation that started with discussion around a strategic initiative with guardrail considerations, to executing the initiative as part of the portfolio, to delivering the initiative to the customer. All done in 54 status changes, or 66 if both epics and sub-epics were used in the runway. We broke the conversation down into three alignment points, Investment, Portfolio, and Delivery, given typical content, resource and effort load considerations, and their effect on flow.

The flow example is intended to illustrate the simplest possible conversation (single initiative, epic, sub-epic, feature, story). Additional work-items needed to deliver minimum viable product will include their own conversation flows as illustrated in *Figure 18.1*. However simplistic, the single work-item flow is always a great way for your alignment point teams to validate and exercise their delivery system.

Flow Design Tip

> Build out your conversation flow, then test it by flowing a single example of all the work-item types developed at each alignment point.

The intent of the workflow representing the conversation was to:

- Eliminate communication gaps while minimally increasing communication load.

- Efficiently organize teams and delivery system around producing value for the company.

- Provide built-in methods for the conversation to continuously improve itself (Waste and Strategic Refactoring taxonomies, actionable analysis of wait states via cycle time and lead time metrics, opportunities for Scrum teams to improve performance).

- Provide means of reciprocation of the agile values of *trust, transparency, commitment, and continuous improvement* as required by cultural contract.

- Provide facilitation of *mastery, autonomy, and purpose* as goal of efficiency in workflow design.

Humans are wired for problem solving agility. In fact, as I show by my infamous "elliptical" example in my Agile Fundamentals class, we're experts at solving problems this way, born with this ability. Individually, all we humans need is an opportunity to instinctively iterate over a challenge, inspecting and adapting along the way.

While we can do this at an instinctive, individual level, the trick is applying what we do instinctively in a collaborative, scalable way, involving hundreds, possibly thousands of people. Conceptually, pretty simple, right? The workflow, taxonomies, and template tools described in this book are an effort to facilitate just that.

That's the path that leads to Agile V2 from Agile V1. Dinosaurs had to swallow rocks to help them digest food – there's got to be a more efficient, anti-fragile way to consume sustenance. So the question is, is it better to continue dedicating substantial time and resources to install a huge agile framework upfront, or is it better to start iterating, inspecting outcomes, and adapting as necessary from a simpler point of view with much lower startup costs, that of the organizational conversation? While both approaches might (eventually) facilitate the ability to compete at market speed, it's likely that the simpler approach will get you there faster, with smaller mistakes, and lower costs along the way. If Agile V1 makes the assumption that we need to build the backlog for the whole transformation scheme upfront, and then spend years trying to attain it, Agile V2 just encourages the minimum viable product required to stay ahead of the competition.

So just as our journey to Agile V2 reveals, start with a simple organizational conversation model (as with our example conversation structure in the book), add complexity in small batches as needed, and provide mechanisms right into the conversational flow that support continuous improvement. *Don't add complexity, unless that complexity is worth the dysfunction it addresses.*

How about this for the first improvement feature included in our example organizational conversation? Use the strategic Refactoring or Waste taxonomies, as described in *Chapter 15*.

Kaizen Feature:
- Current State – Delivery system requires use of PI Planning event.
- Future State – Remote working environment requires organizational conversation be optimized to eliminate need for this stop-the-world event.

Does the conversation structure proposed in this book deliver enough signal from the Investment level to the Portfolio level, to facilitate the Portfolio level's ability to do effective feature handoff to the Delivery level so that PI planning has become redundant?

If yes then great, future state achieved. If no, then keep adding complexity (possibly additional statuses to conversation flow, changes in team topologies) via small batch sizes executed in the improvement taxonomies we already have to make PI Planning redundant. The result is, an expensive wait state has been eliminated in the organizational conversation.

Agile V2 encourages adding complexity in small batches to achieve the right balance of minimal complexity to competitive value generation. While we as coaches encourage our clients to deliver minimum viable product, which in turn maximizes the amount of work not done and creates value as quickly as possible, we aren't as good at taking our own advice. The continuous improvement encouraged by Agile V2 demands we *simplify* and practice *economy of flow* via the delivery systems we design and coach.

If you came to the educated conclusion that PI Planning is still necessary, then at least you will know exactly why, including why this event is part of the cost of doing business. Maybe go back to a *Version Point* in the Investment taxonomy (see *Chapter 11*) and consider a new perspective of the organizational conversation as another strategy for eliminating PI Planning. Don't forget to make use of your built-in improvement taxonomies to structure and track this effort.

The ability to work improvement stories just like any other work-item in the taxonomy is extremely strategic. It means the Agile V2 Organizational Conversation has the *ability to modify itself* using the same way it produces value for the organization. Let's make sure we understand the full implication of that notion.

As seen in *Figure 18.1*, the Agile V2 Organizational Conversation is intended to deliver enough signal to produce value via a *flow* intended to minimize every possible wait state. Generally, events like PI Planning can be deprecated since flow allows conversations to continue without the need for stop-the-world planning events.

Since improvements can be identified and delivered as part of the same flow, improvement conversations can be stewarded in the same fashion, thus deprecating the need for stop-the-world Inspect and Adapt workshops.

Another improvement on the way to Agile V2 is it's direct inclusion of a cultural contract that codifies value reciprocation into the organizational conversation flow. This simplifies greatly the Agile V1 notion of "Agile Transformation" at the cultural level.

It's unfortunate that this notion of Agile Transformation has made its way into the business agility industry's lexicon as a selling point, since the very choice of words discourages replacing the notion with something more efficient and less costly. "Transformation" implies high expectations for change in areas of the organization that can't be changed simply by becoming agile. If existing resources in your organization are already poor project stewards, they'll continue to be so after any so-called agile transformation has taken place.

Additionally, if the transformation is meant to address legacy organizational artifacts like heavy middle management layers and the wait states they cause, or moving from a project to a product driven organization supplemented by agile budget management, that's addressed via strategic refactoring of the organizational conversation.

As good coaches who practice the agile value of continuous improvement, one of the reasons we should be doing these grand-scale agile transformations is to figure out how *not* to do these grand-scale agile transformations. As I've said before, dinosaurs had to swallow rocks to digest food; well, we've built a whole industry around the best ways to swallow rocks, in spite of the fact that this is a fragile, costly, and time consuming approach to survival and organizational competitiveness.

So what I'm proposing in this book is that we explore actually transforming the transformation. Simplify our approach so that we no longer have to achieve rock-swallowing certifications. We've gone through the throes of transforming to Agile V2; now Agile V2 encourages us to start favoring simple refactoring approaches over grand transformation approaches. This is more of a hard skills effort that lends itself to measuring and adapting in a systematic way than a subjective, soft skills effort that might sound great, but yields more nebulous outcomes.

But what about the agile *values* (see *Chapter 8*) necessary to facilitate an efficient organizational conversation? Isn't that the more important aspect of an agile transformation, and how are these values reinforced if not via continual coaching?

What I'd suggest is that reinforcement of cultural values for the purpose of delivering value in the organization is more effective if these values are part of the delivery system structure. As we design or refactor the conversation, let's make sure reciprocation of these values is built right into conversation. The *cultural contract* (see *Chapter 8*) is a great way to do this, and reinforces cultural values becoming individual habits via *repetition of flow*. Values practiced as habits are key traits displayed by any good project steward.

Finally, the cultural traits of "servant leadership" and "mastery, autonomy, and purpose" as they exist in Agile V1 are distilled into this simple principle used in the design of the Agile V2 Organizational Conversation. From *Chapter 7*: *Push the decision making as close as possible to the people delivering the outcomes. A system that encourages this produces higher engagement, leading to better decisions, and faster execution.* Facilitating the conversation in this fashion implicitly codifies these cultural traits into the organization's culture.

So here's a lean-flavored irony that is unlocked by moving to Agile V2: Earlier, I stated, "If the existing resources in your organization are already poor project stewards, they'll continue to be so after any so-called agile transformation has taken place." That's not entirely true. Since the Agile V2 Organizational Conversation codifies the cultural values of trust, transparency, commitment, and continuous improvement, along with mastery, autonomy, and purpose right into its flow, resources who continue to be poor project stewards will likely "be voted off the island" by their colleagues.

Lean Agile V2

> Trust the process you and your team created; the Agile V1 details you had to track before will be taken care of implicitly.

So let's begin the organizational conversation. Why not start with discussion regarding the conversation structure itself? *Emulate* the structure suggested in this book, *Embrace* and understand the techniques and intent of the templates and alignment points, then *Establish* your own organizational conversation. Start simple, iterate, adapt; only add complexity when that complexity is worth the dysfunction it addresses. Remember, it's just a conversation...

ABOUT THE AUTHOR

James Smith started his career 33 years ago as a software developer for a small company called TAPSCAN, now famous as a pioneer of media sales applications. From there, he's held many titles, from architect, to manager, to VP and CTO. Back in 2003, James wrote the first hybrid certified mail system and website hosted by the US Postal Service.

Along the way, James began examining how businesses structure their delivery systems to provide value. That effort led him to exploring business agility and process engineering, reading books and papers from thought leaders like Reinertsen, Leffingwell, Sutherland, with heavy influence from Edwards Deming, and many others. While James continues to actively engage clients as Agile

Coach and Consultant, his learnings have led him more in the direction of business systems engineering, descended from the grand discipline of Industrial Engineering.

Most recently, James has spent the bulk of his professional time consulting for state government and F200 corporations.

Even though James no longer writes code for customers, he's working on several personal startup efforts, including a new corporate backlog workflow management application that helps organizations move from Agile V1 to Agile V2.

For questions, inquiries, or information regarding Agile V2 seminars, feel free to reach out to James at jksmith@increasesignal.com or by visiting Increase Signal Corporation.

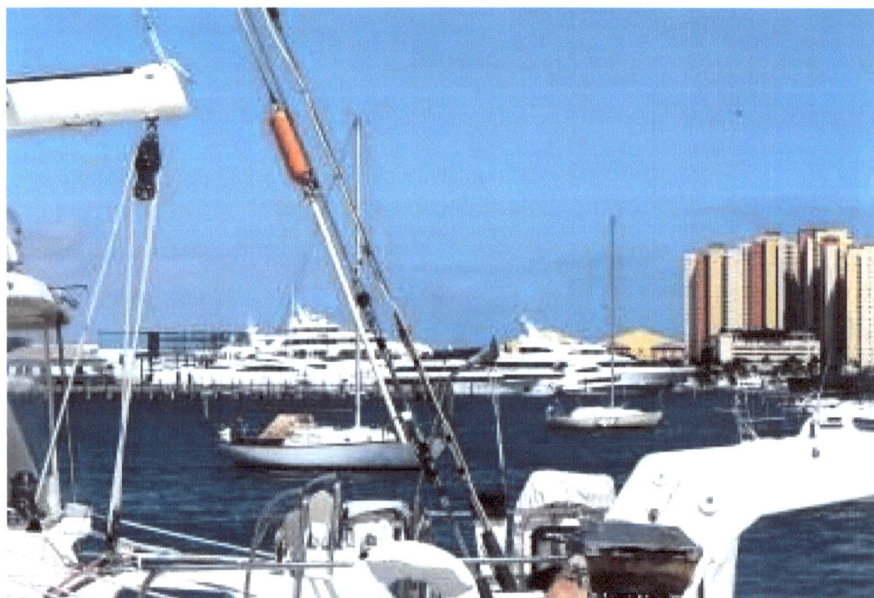

Riviera Beach Marina, West Palm Beach, March 13, 2019

ANSWERS TO EXERCISE QUESTIONS

1) In *Figure 9.2*, how many constraint buffers does the Kanban board have versus the Scrum board? (Read up on constraint buffers and Theory of Constraints).

The Kanban board in the figure has two constraint buffers, "To Do" and "Ready To Test." The Scrum board is also a Kanban board, but in its simplest form as a board accommodating only one speed. The "To Do" status is the only constraint buffer on the Scrum board.

Active states on a Kanban board can all represent constraints and different board speeds. Those constraints can be less disruptive to flow with judicious use of WIP limits and "Ready To" statuses in front of those constraints.

2) Why is Scrum always expected to have a cycle-time of one iteration and a flow efficiency of 100%? (*refer to* *Figure 9.2*).

The primary concern of Scrum is not to make teams feel more productive, but to provide the organization with a predictable execution process to deliver the portfolio. While Scrum requires much more administration and is less flexible than its parent, Kanban, a mature Scrum team will deliver all promised increments of work every iteration. A Scrum board can be measured just like a Kanban board using cycle time and flow efficiency, but since all stories are delivered every iteration, those measurements will be constant, while only velocity might change.

3) Why should your Scrum board not have a "Ready To Test" or "Test" status?

"Test" statuses just encourage unnecessary wait states and introduce complication into the Scrum process, which is designed to be very simple and with only one board speed. If testing is included simultaneously as part of the "In Progress" development activities, this will give the Scrum team the best chance for meeting sprint commitments by keeping development mistakes smaller and minimize the chance of escaped defects.

Additionally, don't confuse general testing with PO acceptance testing. The PO has committed to attend sprint review on a specific date and time when stories will be demonstrated and accepted according to PO requirements. PO's have enough to do just keeping high performing Scrum teams fed with a healthy backlog, so depending on them to do individual testing during the sprint can jeopardize sprint commitments.

4) How would you describe "holding costs" and "transaction (administrative) costs" for each process? Check out this video on optimal batch sizes for clues.

In short, holding costs for a work-item increase when it takes too long to move that item from one status to the next. Then process flow gets clogged and status speed slows down. This of course can spike board cycle time and is an indicator that work-item batch size should be smaller.

Transaction (administration) costs can increase when work-item batch sizes are so small they overwhelm the process. This can be addresses by adding more automation to the process or increasing batch size. For instance, pulling stories estimated with a size of 1 into a sprint is not efficient, since Scrum is already heavily laden with administration costs. It would be best to combine some of those 1-point stories to create a larger story.

5) How would you calculate the Lead Time for this initiative in your head? (Hint: Read the rest of the book for the answer.)

(See Figure 18.1) As each story is delivered to customer, update Status 54. Once all stories are delivered to customer, update Status 40. Once all features are delivered to customer, update Status 24, once all epics are delivered, update Status 12.

6) Why do dependencies have to be eliminated in the Scrum process, but not in Kanban?

Scrum needs to provide every guarantee that stories in a sprint will be delivered by the end of that sprint. That means story delivery must be wholly owned by the Scrum team. External dependencies aren't owned by the Scrum team, therefore, delivery of any story that has external dependencies cannot be owned by the Scrum team. See INVEST criteria to understand what characteristics a Scrum-able story should have.

Kanban doesn't have the same requirement, and in fact has no set prescription. This more flexible parent of Scrum can track development progress on any kind of work-item via cycle time and flow efficiency. But Kanban also provides no mechanisms to help teams commit to completion of stories in the same way Scrum does.

7) Why should expected velocity generally be driven by velocity of the team's last sprint instead of an average of prior sprints?

Averages of any number run the risk of hiding dysfunction, and part of the strength of a good Scrum process is that it surfaces dysfunction. Besides, using averages just to make teams look better overall is a denial of the agile value of transparency. In practice, a good Scrum team couldn't care less about the velocity they report at any given time. If the team has been on holiday after an abbreviated sprint, the PO knows simply to bring that many more stories as stretch goals to the next sprint review. Perhaps the team can catch back up in one or two sprints. Whatever the case, still use the velocity from the last sprint to provide the most reliable indicator of what can be done in the next sprint.

8) Why should sprint burn-down charts be measured in task hours instead of story points?

Using story points in a sprint burn down instead of task hours hides possible sprint dysfunction and might make it too late in the sprint to activate emergency procedures if necessary.

As explained in *Chapter 17*, any task estimates made in hours (such as with Implementation Plans and Capacity Plans) are for the eyes of the Scrum team only.

LINKS

Essential Scrum	https://www.amazon.com/Essential-Scrum-Practical-Addison-Wesley-Signature/dp/0137043295
Conway's Law	https://www.melconway.com/Home/Conways_Law.html
Accelerate: The Science of Lean Software and Dev Ops	https://www.amazon.com/Accelerate-Software-Performing-Technology-Organizations-ebook/dp/B07B9F83WM
Chesterton's fence	https://en.wikipedia.org/wiki/Wikipedia:Chesterton's_fence
The Design Squiggle	https://thedesignsquiggle.com/
Daniel Pink	https://www.danpink.com/
Optimal Batch Sizes	https://increasesignal.com/videos/OptBatch.mp4
Prioritizing Work-Items	https://increasesignal.com/videos/PrioritizeWorkItems.mp4
Objectives and Key Results (OKR's)	https://en.wikipedia.org/wiki/OKR
Tiger team	https://en.wikipedia.org/wiki/Tiger_team
Scientific method	https://www.sciencebuddies.org/science-fair-projects/science-fair/steps-of-the-scientific-method
Constraint buffers	https://en.wikipedia.org/wiki/Theory_of_constraints

Constraint buffer	https://www.accountingtools.com/articles/2017/5/15/the-constraint-buffer
Kaizen (Improvement)	https://en.wikipedia.org/wiki/Kaizen
Software Development Performance Index (SDPI)	https://techdocs.broadcom.com/content/broadcom/techdocs/us/en/ca-enterprise-software/agile-development-and-management/rally-platform-ca-agile-central/rally/reporting-top/rally-insights-overview/insights-performance-index-calculation.html
Industrial Engineering	https://en.wikipedia.org/wiki/Industrial_engineering
INVEST Criteria	https://xp123.com/articles/invest-in-good-stories-and-smart-tasks/
Lean-Agile Immersion Example for Divisions and Product Lines	https://increasesignal.com/immersion.pdf

FIGURES

CONCLUDING UNSCIENTIFIC POSTSCRIPT TO PHILOSOPHICAL FRAGMENTS*

As I was finishing the book, this notion of "transforming the transformation" as a progression from Agile V1 to Agile V2 kept nagging at me. I wanted to provide something more actionable than just making a high-minded statement about what we need to do to refactor our dogmatic loyalty to this industry mantra of "agile transformation."

Then I woke up one morning thinking about one particularly heavy agile framework being like one of my early software projects. That project was done in waterfall fashion without the benefit of *test-driven development*. The result was an effort that took at least two years longer and produced a much lower ROI than it should have because the project didn't adhere to a number of simple notions we take for granted in agile software development:

- Our scope was fixed and lived in a specification, a common waterfall development characteristic. Minimum viable product and 80/20 rule prioritization were definitely not a concern, so development costs were about as high as they could get.

- We did no test-driven development. Along with fixed scope, we probably ended up writing and testing about 50% more code than we should have to get to market.

My company still made money on the resulting product, mainly because the one other competitor was also playing by the same rules. But organizations don't have this luxury anymore. Competition is much more fierce, and development timelines have compressed thanks to observations about how products are used, as well as development practices like TDD. Agile practices encouraging minimum viable product, maximizing the amount of work not done, along with writing the least amount of tested code necessary to deliver valuable product increments are the rule of the day for competitive organizations.

And it occurred to me that while we make use of these practices in our system of delivery, we don't always do a good job of executing the same in our system of transformation. Why aren't transformations test driven with an emphasis on minimum viable product in the spirit of contributing to organizational competitiveness as quickly as possible?

This system of delivery and system of transformation combine to form the organization's *system of competitiveness*. If either system is weak, that organization will not be as competitive as it could be.

So instead of a test-driven approach with specific acceptance criteria, we attempt to apply these heavy, out-of-box frameworks in combination with cultural organizational changes pitched in broad, subjective terms. Fatigue sets in from these agile transformation efforts, lasting years and costing millions of dollars.

For some organizations, at least on the framework side, the response is to throw out the heavy framework in favor of something like Spotify. But this approach works for Spotify the organization; I've never heard anyone from Spotify suggest that their agile approach was meant to be general purpose for any organization. And with a SaaS revenue model, Spotify's requirements for organizing around value, including measuring and reporting that value, are infinitely simpler than that of Ford Motor or a highly sophisticated technology behemoth like Ernst and Young. Just to pick this model because SAFe is too heavy is a strategic mistake. Decisions about framework approach must be more coherent than that.

Calling a more considered approach (you guessed it) *Test Driven Transformation,* let's start with our basic organizational conversation framework. This includes built-in ways for the framework to improve itself, as well as codify the agile values (trust, transparency, commitment, and continuous improvement), along with codification of mastery, autonomy, and purpose. Use the bullets stated in *Chapter 18* as minimal acceptance tests for transformation value.

We've distilled our cognitive load down to simple trust in the process we designed for our organization. We've leaned out our communication channels for increasing efficiency. We've adjusted our team topologies as necessary. We've applied Kanban and Scrum not just as our teams prefer, but for the health of the whole organizational conversation, given the signal available at any instance as the conversation flows. Nothing out of a box and no framework specific certifications required. And we did all this by applying a system that helps us add more complexity, only when the complexity is needed and useful. That's what Agile V2 is all about.

James K Smith
September 18, 2020
Miami Beach

Thanks to the 19th century philosopher Soren Kierkegaard for his piece titled the same. As a professor used to tell me, "Don't be a Soren."

APPENDIX

Bal Harbour, Oct 3, 2020

FUN AND PROFIT WITH FLOW CALCULATIONS

Cycle Time and Lead Time as shown in the workflows in this manual are calculated as per work-item. But if you have a coherent workflow mapped for your entire organizational conversation as you should, it's valuable to calculate CT and LT based on overall production workflow as well.

It's also valuable to calculate CT for any arbitrary slice of the conversation workflow. Here's a use case for such a need:

1. Status in your flow has an external dependency on user acceptance testing.
2. User acceptance testing (UAT) is taking so long that it's having a detrimental impact on work-item cycle times.
3. To reveal different speeds in your workflow, you choose to measure CT from "Ready For Dev" to "Ready for UAT," then from "In UAT" to "Done."
4. Measurement reveals a flow showing a substantial spike in cycle time and decrease in production speed beginning with the "In UAT" status. We should focus our efforts for increased efficiency and elimination of waste at this area of the workflow.

Examining the speed of portions of your workflow is just as important as CT per work-item. Here's an illustration: Your CT per work-item is high, so you decide to make your stories smaller, or split existing stories, with the intent of lowering CT by reducing effort to complete each story.

As Reinertsen points out in his authoritative reference, "The

Principles of Product Development Flow," workflows respond well to smaller batch sizes. And that will be reflected in per work-item CT. But what do we have to watch out for if we start splitting stories just to game our performance metrics? Does the effort raise the risk of higher effort overhead required from PO activities? Does the administration cost (testing, deployment) for each story remain generally the same no matter what your story size? If so for either question, flow costs might increase for the same measurement interval.

So, at some point, reducing batch sizes just to lower work-item CT will yield diminishing returns. Instead of the smallest possible batch size, look for optimal batch sizes with an eye toward delivery of value and workflow limitations. Besides calculating work-item CT and LT, also calculating CT and LT for the whole production workflow over a particular time interval will help you tune batch sizes for an optimal value stream.

Here's how to calculate production workflow for a particular time interval: Pick the starting and ending statuses on your workflow that you'd like to measure. The ending status you've chosen for this measurement is, for all intents, your throughput status. Determine the WIP in the workflow across all the statuses, including starting and ending status. Whether you count WIP in items or points, divide that value by everything in your throughput status. If you use the same time interval repeatedly, the CT you calculated would be expressed in "X" time intervals.

Test this calculation with a Scrum board. In this case, your interval will be a single sprint or iteration. At the end of the sprint, if WIP on the whole board is divided by throughput (or "Done"), what ideally should your production workflow CT be? Your calculation should yield the value "1," as in Done divided by Done. If the number is larger than one sprint, then the sprint is will have one or more unfinished stories.

In truth, while optimizing batch sizes for flow is always of value, taking actions that directly address CT and LT may not be as helpful as you'd hope. Don't immediately jump to getting your teams to splitting stories, along with the incurring wait states like story sizing workshops and the like. Chances are far more likely that your team's Definition of Ready is just weak, so the team is accepting poorly defined stories in the first place. Splitting a poorly defined story will create two smaller, but still poorly defined stories; now your administration costs just went up.

The best solutions for reducing CT and LT are not necessarily obvious. Process flow as executed by humans can be like jazz music. Look behind the notes for other than what's expected.

COST PER STORY POINT/COST PER SPRINT

Now that we have a more comprehensive understanding for measuring cycle time and lead time, let's get serious about cost to produce value for our whole organizational conversation. Using the templates, we are now capable of producing a CT and LT per work item cost for any of the work-items in our taxonomy.

If those work-items are stories delivered via scrum, calculate cost per story point at the end of each sprint, like so:

CPSP for Sprint X = (Operating Cost of a Team for a Sprint) / (Velocity for that same Sprint)

If the work-items are delivered using kanban, use of story points or iterations is not prescribed for that process. This calculation, like CT, is done on an arbitrary measurement interval. So calculate cost per story point (or cost per card) at the end of each interval, like so:

CPSP for Interval X = (Operating Cost of a Team for an Interval) / (Throughput for that Interval)

If used in combination with the conversation structure described in this book, these cost metrics can surface the cost to deliver a whole strategic initiative, or any sub-portion of that initiative all the way to delivery to customer. Now your CFO is armed with granular historicals that can be used to guide continuous, lean budgeting in the future.

UNVARNISHED NOTES FOR
ORGANIZATIONAL LEADERSHIP

Based on my transformation engagement experiences with large organizations, I see a couple of recurring themes on a regular basis:

1) While organizations address their sustainability needs with full-time employee resources, they often make use of agencies to provide a pool of agile coaches to facilitate their initial agile transformation efforts. These coaches represent a broad array of experiences and skill sets. Except for some basics, they may not display any alignment at all, even within the same agency.

2) Even with an organizational mandate to transform or just simply refactor, when faced with meeting hard dates handed down from leadership, managers are quick to throw lean-agile potential gains out the window. They revert to the usual act of throwing globs of poorly defined initiatives to delivery teams, then telling the teams to just do what they need to do to meet the dates. Then they micro-manage the teams on the back-end because necessary progression to those dates is not proceeding as planned.

And of course the familiar story plays out. The teams are pushed into overtime mode, team utilization goes up, work queues grow, cycle time increases, defects start escaping, good practices and habits go by the wayside, stories that don't meet the definition of ready are pulled into sprints, and so on. Then leadership ends up spending more time micro-managing defect resolution to get releases out the door instead of doing what they should be doing, which is facilitating the ability of delivery teams to pull the kind signal they need to execute on with confidence to deliver working, tested minimum viable product.

Coaching teams are then employed like a checkbox (from the transformation checklist) to improve the situation. But the coaching teams operate coherently only in the most basic way. Playbooks and improvement approaches aren't aligned; overall coaching effectiveness is marginal.

Tossing out a lean-agile system of delivery and accompanying best practices in favor of managing delivery teams to meet dates ends up causing the opposite of what was intended. Dates slip, and outcomes are devalued and defects increase as time passes.

Leadership, here's what your management has lost sight of, or simply doesn't understand: Delivering value in the most lean and agile way possible is the most effective treatment for dealing with the pathological dysfunction of chasing delivery dates. *The more lean and agile your organizational value conversation becomes, the closer this conversation gets to delivering value in the fastest way possible, for every instance of every product.* Scope becomes minimum viable product. Delivery date becomes whenever the organizational conversation delivers, given minimum viable product and execution done with a healthy sense of urgency.

I can't emphasize this enough. Don't refactor your organization in a lean-agile way because agile transformation is a popular thing to do. Don't even refactor your organization because the effort makes for happier, more fulfilled employees. Refactor and continuously improve your organization so you can *stop chasing delivery dates.* You want an organizational conversation that reveals delivery dates instead of forcing a conversation to meet those dates.

It's like getting across town by catching most of the greenlights*. And the more efficient your delivery system gets, the more greenlights* you'll discover.

So if you want to build a more lean-agile organization, how do you avoid the revolting predicament I described above? Start by framing your organizational transformation or refactoring with these simple pointers:

- Understand this is just an organizational conversation that produces value. Don't add complexity unless the complexity is worth the dysfunction it addresses. Boxed frameworks often add gratuitous complexity that's unnecessary.

- Model the conversation structure in a taxonomy. Don't commit to this effort half-ass. Get your v1 taxon together and start iterating over it to improve or grow as justified.

- Insert alignment points as teams into the conversation structure that use this taxonomy to decrease noise and increase signal for the next alignment point in the conversation flow. Be sensitive to team cognitive and communication loads. This is your v1 organizational conversation. Use your built-in improvement mechanisms (did you read the book?) to increase the effectiveness and efficiency of the conversation. Don't do this half-ass.

- Make sure your coaches are competent business systems engineers who can help you validate your conversation flow and the taxon it will operate on. Also make sure your coaches form their own system of transformation alignment point represented by a uniform playbook based on best practices, habits, and training that feed productivity, predictability, and quality. A half-ass coaching team will end up being an expensive checkbox, and that's it.

- Fully engage and operationalize organizational leadership as an alignment point with their part of the taxonomy at the beginning of the conversation. They must commit to not doing this work half-ass. Leadership leads the charge and sets an example by allowing their portion of the conversation flow to be measured for efficiency just as every other part of the conversation is measured. See the example taxonomy leadership would be responsible for in the book.

- Operationalize for each division or product line with a 30-40 hour immersion training that covers their part of the organizational conversation. See links table for link to immersion example. Don't do this half-ass.

So you get the point. Don't approach developing and operationalizing your organizational value conversation in a half-ass way. If so, fragility follows. Perhaps even worse, don't let your management execute the conversation in a half-ass manner, either because they think it's too much trouble or they think following the conversation impedes their ability to meet hard dates. Going down this management hole sets conversation execution up for failure.

Like a successful professional sports team, a great organization not only trusts their process, they love it.

That's your winning culture, and it's a pretty simple ask I'm making of you at this point. From leadership to delivery team, from sales to prodops, your people must love, own and nurture the flow of your organizational delivery conversation. Don't do this stuff half-ass; strive for excellence of execution. Starting at the leadership level, use the templates and techniques described in this book to implement the simple pointers stated above, and your organization will become increasingly competitive.

Greenlights by Matthew McConaughey. He describes a greenlight as more than just a green traffic light. "A greenlight is an affirmation, setting yourself up for success." In lean fashion, McConaughey also managed to shorten the spelling while expanding the value of the phrase.

5000 years of boat technology. Miami Beach, April 2020

www.ingramcontent.com/pod-product-compliance
Lightning Source LLC
Chambersburg PA
CBHW041314210326
41599CB00008B/266